THOMAS MERTON

GEORGE WOODCOCK

THOMAS MERTON

MONK AND POET

A Critical Study

Canongate

EDINBURGH

Contents

Introduction

To those who are neither monks nor poets there has always seemed a central contradiction — or even a series of contradictions — in the life of Thomas Merton: in what, if he had been a secular man, we would call his career. The images that emerge of him seem often bewilderingly multiple. There is the hermit, seeking the silence and solitude where truth comes to one and God seeks one out; and there is the celebrated and industrious man of letters, with more than half a hundred books to his credit, hundreds of articles and reviews, and a mail so heavy that in his later years he would go down from his hermitage to the main buildings of his abbey with a suitcase to carry it back. When one looks farther into his life, the contradictions appear to multiply indefinitely: the contemplative who proclaims the necessity of the desert shows himself a man deeply concerned over questions of social justice in the world he left; the devoted Catholic emerges not only as an enthusiastic advocate of the Christian ecumenism proclaimed in the historic Church Council we know as Vatican II but also as a searcher in Asian religious traditions for parallel ways towards the transcendence of the self.

In fact, the contradictions are more apparent than real. Perhaps one could describe them as differing facets, looking often in opposing directions, of a single conception of existence and of the human soul. Many more ways than one exist of losing one's ordinary, worldly self. Perhaps the simplest, for Merton, was that which he took when he left secular life and became the obedient cenobitic monk who followed a traditional path into the priesthood and was known in his community as Father Louis. Another, and not an incompatible way, was the solitary path of contemplation leading to the sense of mystical encounter with the unknowable God. But — as poets and other artists know — the act of artistic or intellectual creation can be yet another form of self-abnegation. The creative persona is not the self as commonly understood; he is a different being from the man with the same name whom the world encounters in the street or at the bank; his creative powers enter him and manifest themselves as mysteriously as the contemplative's intuitions. Some writers have recognized this fact by assuming different names under which to publish their works, less out of modesty than from the sense of another voice speaking within them. Eric Blair, who became George Orwell, is perhaps the most celebrated modern example. There is, indeed, more than an analogical relationship between being reborn into the life of creation and being reborn into spiritual life. Thus in the mature Merton we can perhaps see a trio of beings existing, different but without conflict: Father Louis, who carried on the monastic and priestly duties; the nameless hermit who had gone like the ancient eremitic fathers into the desert of contemplation (in physical terms a cinder-block cottage in the woods of his abbey in Kentucky); and the creative writer who for convenience retained the secular name of a past self, and whom the wider world knew. These three Mertons lived in harmony because they sustained each other and were in fact the aspects of a single whole, a human if distant reflection of the Trinity.

It was perhaps because most of the world saw only one of the three Mertons, the poet and religious writer whose work formed such a clear yet such a unique window on the monastic mind, that the idea of conflict and contradiction arose, to Merton's own frequent distress. "Many rumors have been disseminated about me since I came to the monastery," he said in 1963, writing a preface to the Japanese edition of *The Seven Storey Mountain*. "Most of them have assured people that I had left the monastery, that I had returned to New York, that I was in Europe, that I was in South

America or Asia, that I had become a hermit, that I was married, that I was drunk, that I was dead." Of the rumours some indeed came true, though not in the way their disseminators intended, for when Merton did become a hermit it was within the setting of his beloved Abbey of Gethsemani, and when he did indeed go to Asia — and there died — it was in the hope of finding the common elements between his own contemplative tradition and similar traditions within Asian religions and of strengthening his Christian monasticism.

Equally unreal is the division that may at first appear between the contemplative and the man of intense and radical social concern whom Merton showed himself to be in the 1960s. Contemplatives have not always been men who detached themselves wholly from the world. In *Ends and Means* and in *The Perennial Philosophy,* two books which influenced Merton's early intellectual development, Aldous Huxley argued that the world could be saved from destruction by war and civil conflict only if men stilled their minds and nurtured their spirits in the contemplative life. There are many instances of lay contemplatives or mystics who have shown remarkable insight and even practical capability in the affairs of the ordinary world; William Blake and the Irish poet George Russell ("AE") are examples that immediately come to mind. Merton himself was deeply impressed by the way in which a contemplative bent turned the simple and gentle Shakers not only into a peaceful community but also into craftsmen of remarkable sureness and sensibility. Merton also admired Gandhi, preparing for publication a selection of his sayings on non-violence, and here was perhaps the most striking example in history of the combination of a spiritual life with the liberatory politics which it irradiated; it was other men's lack of inner light that made Gandhi's achievement seem in the end a failure.

Unlike his friend Dan Berrigan, whose Jesuit vocation predisposed him to activism, Merton did not feel impelled to become involved in political deeds. The monk's duty, he believed, was rather to cultivate consciousness and awareness, and at the same time to be ideologically uncommitted (which did not mean ignoring ideologies, for Merton was an attentive reader of Marx and Marcuse); "... *the monk should be the man in the Church who is*

not organized but is free with the freedom of the desert nomad."
(*Contemplation in a World of Action:* Merton's italics)

But such consciousness, such awareness, such freedom, laid
the obligation to speak out in a world in crisis, and not only to
proclaim the positive nature of love but also to expose the spiritual
sickness of the Eichmanns whose errors of omission and commission
become objectified in actions of world-shaking evil. "It is my intention," Merton said, "to make my entire life a rejection of, a
protest against the crimes and injustices of war and political tyranny." But he also, in *Raids on the Unspeakable* (1966), restated
the Huxleyan arguments that had influenced him a quarter of a
century before by saying that only the spiritually realized "can live
without the need to kill, and without the need of a doctrine that
permits him to do so with good conscience" and that it is the solitary "(whether in the city or the desert) who does mankind the
inestimable favor of reminding it of its true capacity for maturity,
liberty and peace." And though he talked in his last days, at the
Calcutta conference shortly before his death in 1968, of the monk
as a "very strange kind of person, a marginal person," and by
implication ranked him near to those other marginal persons who
in the counter culture of that time were posing their alternatives
to an acquisitive and violent society, Merton never showed any
sign of moving out of the role of a Christian monk. Once he remarked that if he had not chosen the monastic life, conscience
would have made him an anarchist; but it was the monastic life
he chose and to which he remained dedicated. On this point he
was still as certain when he died as he had been five years before
when, in introducing the Japanese translation of *The Seven Storey
Mountain,* he remarked: "I have never for a moment thought of
changing the definitive decisions taken in the course of my life: to
be a Christian, to be a monk, to be a priest."

But being a Christian and a monk and a priest did not involve
closing oneself to other traditions, or to other variants of Christianity than the Catholicism to which Merton remained so unques-
tioningly faithful. It is true that in early works like *The Seven
Storey Mountain* and *Seeds of Contemplation* there is a certain
callow zealotry, a narrowness and intolerance of approach. Father
Aldhelm Cameron-Brown aptly described the first work as "that

swan-song of the nineteenth-century monastic revival," while *Seeds of Contemplation*—unlike its 1962 successor *New Seeds of Contemplation*—suggests that there is only one valid contemplative tradition, that embodied in the variant practices of Catholic monastic orders.

Merton's mind and his nature were too expansive to remain long in so narrow a mould. Twenty years later he could look back on *The Seven Storey Mountain* and say that "since that time, I have learned—I believe—to look upon the world with more compassion," and round about the same time, completing his book on the great Taoist master, *The Way of Chuang Tzu,* he could remark that he "had enjoyed writing this book more than any other I can remember."

Merton was one of the earliest to catch the mood of ecumenism which in 1962 was so dramatically exemplified in Vatican II; he seemed by this time to be awaiting some such expansion of the Catholic outlook like dry earth awaiting rain. "Openness to the world," he declared in the posthumously published *Contemplation in a World of Action,* "is demanded by the realization that the world of today, in which man's whole future for good or for evil now rests in his own hands, is for all men the place of God's epiphany as Judge and as Savior, as the Lord of History." And a few years earlier, in *Conjectures of a Guilty Bystander,* he talked passionately of the reuniting of all Christians.

> If I can unite *in myself* the thought and the devotion of Eastern and Western Christendom, the Greek and the Latin Fathers, the Russians with the Spanish mystics, I can prepare in myself the reunion of divided Christians. From that secret and unspoken unity in myself can eventually come a visible and manifest unity of all Christians. If we want to bring together what is divided, we can not do so by imposing one division upon the other or absorbing one division into the other. But if we do this, the union is not Christian. It is political, and doomed to further conflict. We must contain all divided worlds in ourselves and transcend them in Christ.

During the 1960s Merton went beyond the reunion of Christians towards a wider understanding between Christians and men of other faiths and even men without—in the conventional sense—

faith at all. His essays on Zen and Taoism are among his most poetic and sympathetic works, perhaps because here he was in no way bound by the dogmas of a church he himself upheld; he wrote with understanding on the Sufis and other non-Christian mystics. In doing so he was returning to an interest of his pre-monastic young manhood in Eastern religions and concepts of living which projected a concern for self-transcendence similar to his own. By 1965 he was saying, in *Contemplation in a World of Action,*

> In a certain sense the duty to bear witness to contemplative values, and to a higher experience, is a matter of universal concern, common not only to the Cistercian monk but to the Zen Buddhist and the student of Yoga. We find that many who do not share our religious belief, men of the great Asian religions, or even modern Westerners without faith, tend to have a better appreciation of our life than some Catholics. These men often deeply value the advantages of solitude, silence and meditation. The appeals of such men urge us to persevere in our aim of seeking new depths of awareness and meaning in human existence. They also encourage us to study the ways in which the religious experience of the great mystical traditions, both Christian and non-Christian, can continue in dialogue in a world that has ceased to understand the classic language of religious experience. They encourage us to approach closer to the mystery of God in that desert solitude which is the place par excellence of revelation, inspiration and renewal.

It was in search of the two complementary — rather than contradictory — goals which marked the final years of his life that Thomas Merton set out on the Asian journey which ended when he died in Bangkok: a renewal and extension of Cistercian monasticism, and a dialogue in their own world with representatives of Asian contemplative traditions, no matter what their specific religious orientations. But, as the above quotation suggests, Merton by this time was extending his enquiries and his sympathies beyond those who might be regarded as representatives of established spiritual traditions — even traditions so eccentric as those of Zen or Sufism. Among existentialist and near-existentialist writers like Jean-Paul Sartre and Albert Camus he found appealing resonances despite their rejection of institutionalized religion, and he spoke sympathetically of "the atheist's intuition that God is not an object of limited and precise knowledge." Many who called themselves atheists—he believed—might be "very intrigued by the direct and existential testimony of contemplative experience." In all this Merton was obeying what he saw in his last years as the "life of freedom and detachment," the "marginal" or "desert" existence to which the monk was called. It was a desert that, like Blake's grain of sand, contained a world.

It is from another side of the dialogue and perhaps of the desert that I approach Merton, encouraged inevitably by his own openness to other attitudes, other dispositions. But participation in the dialogue would hardly be possible if there were not some common standing ground, some shared stretch of the desert, such as I believe Merton himself found with all those who had earned his candour and respect.

I am not a Catholic; I am not even a practising Christian, and though I acknowledge the unknowable God, I suspect that my personal kind of deism might come near to what Merton thought of as atheism. Yet there are areas where understanding may flourish. Like Merton I am a poet and have continued lifelong in that craft. Like him, I have also known and discoursed with Asian Buddhists, in Ceylon, in Thailand and especially with the Tibetans in exile, yet without attempting to ape them or to graft their ways of life or thought incongruously onto my own. It is their insights into the common human predicament that I have valued, as Merton did, and their intuitions regarding its transcendence. I share Merton's pacifism, and my rejection of political power is more radical even than his. The limitations of doctrinal agreement between us are evident; the sympathy of approach will also, I hope, be equally evident. I trust I shall show myself as appreciative of Merton's virtues—even when I disagree with him—as he showed himself of the virtues of the Taoist Chuang Tzu and the Zen poet Basho.

George Woodcock
Vancouver, 1978

1

The Life

It has been said that the lives of writers are dull, and the better the writer, the duller the life. In the sense that a dedicated writer is usually too busy at his craft for a multitude of adventures in the external world, this is doubtless true, and it is all the more true when the writer takes the ultimate step into reclusion that makes him first a monk and then a hermit. One could say of Thomas Merton that, however productive and internally active his life may have been, externally it was, for at least the later and the more creative half, remarkably uneventful.

Merton was a child of the period when Europe and the world began to move into the long era of political and social, cultural and eventually religious crisis through which it has been passing for the last two generations. He was born in 1915, on the last day of January. Owen Merton, his father, was a New Zealander who had taken to painting and who eventually gained some repute as a kind of neo-impressionist, selling his work well in Britain and the United States and earning the approval of critics as distinguished as Roger Fry. His mother, born Ruth Jenkins and also a painter, was an American of Quaker faith and Welsh ancestry, a woman of austere temper which may well have been accentuated during Merton's childhood by the cancer from which she eventually died when he was six years old.

The Merton family was living at Prades in the French Pyrenees when Thomas was born, but the circumstances of the war scattered the little Anglo-American society of artists to which they belonged, and in 1916 they returned to the United States, where the younger son, John Paul, was born. Merton's first memories, then, were of rural Long Island, but he was destined to a roving youth. The family moved to Douglaston in New York State, and then, after his mother died, Thomas went with his father to Bermuda, where he began his education in the local elementary school for white children: an ironic commencement for one who in later years became so fervent an advocate of the elimination of all racial barriers.

Two years later, in 1923, the Mertons returned to Douglaston, and the biennial pattern repeated itself, for in 1925 they went on to France, to the Languedoc, where Thomas was partly fascinated by the rich relics of a past mediaeval culture — a fascination that would continue in his later years — and partly appalled and frightened by the brutality he encountered when he was sent as a boarder to the Lycée in Montauban. It seemed a great liberation, another two years later, when in 1929 his father took him to England.

There he first attended a middle-class preparatory school in the London suburbs. His final secondary schooling was taken in the minute and intensely rural county of Rutland, at Oakham School, one of those ancient and struggling English scholastic establishments which claim their place in the lower ranks of the public school system. In 1931 his father died with great fortitude of a brain tumour. Merton continued at Oakham, spending his holidays with his godfather and guardian, a Harley Street specialist who introduced him to modern painting and to the novelists of the inter-war years — Huxley and Gide and Hemingway and Jules Romains. His schoolmasters had already made him familiar with the poets, with Eliot and Hopkins, and he discovered William Blake for himself, so that a basic pattern of literary influences was already being established while he was still at school.

In 1933 Merton won a scholarship to Clare College in Cambridge, and, after a summer in Italy, he took up his studies of modern languages in the intervals of a life mainly dedicated, with a thoroughness that would characterize everything Merton undertook, to hard-drinking frivolity. Somewhat surprisingly, he gained a Second at the end of the year, but his godfather, who had originally suggested he train for the British diplomatic service, decided that the temptations of Cambridge undergraduate life were too compelling, and suggested that Merton return to his mother's parents in New York. At this time, since his father had never taken out American citizenship, Thomas was a British subject, and he appears to have contemplated originally a career in England or in some corner of the Empire, but his return to American soil in December 1934 was decisive; henceforward he would live and work in the United States.

By this time Merton, like many another generous-hearted youth, had succumbed to the political fevers of the Thirties and considered himself a Marxist. He contemplated enrolling in the left-wing New School of Social Research rather than in an ordinary academic institution. But, though he persisted in his radical inclinations so far as to become for a brief period a card-carrying Communist with a party name (Frank Swift), he actually joined Columbia University and studied social sciences until Mark van Doren, one of the great early influences on his life, persuaded him to return to literature.

At Columbia, Merton again lived what he later regarded as an essentially pagan life, becoming an energetic fraternity man and such a hard drinker and smoker that he had to abandon the athletics to which in the beginning he devoted himself. Yet he found time to study, to take his B.A. in 1938 and his M.A. the following year. His thesis, perhaps predictably, was on William Blake, from studying whom he first acquired that fascination with the contemplative way which later so dominated his life.

The year before the thesis on Blake was completed, Merton was converted to Catholicism. Undoubtedly many influences worked hard to bring him to this point. They included some of the men who taught him at Columbia, and especially Daniel Walsh, under whom he studied Thomas Aquinas and his beloved Duns Scotus and the other scholastic philosophers. Also, surging up from the past, there were the memories of the ancient churches and monasteries that had enthralled him as a child in France, and of the moving experience that Rome had been for him in the summer of 1933. And, understandably crucial in the conversion of a man whose Catholicism became inextricably mingled with his vocation as a writer, there were the books that Merton noted down in November 1941, just before he entered Gethsemani, in the last pages of the diary that was eventually published in 1959 as *The Secular Journal*.

> *November 27, 1941.*
>
> I spent most of the afternoon writing a letter to Aldous Huxley and when I finished I thought: 'Who am I to be telling this guy about mysticism?' I reflect that until I read his book, *Ends and Means*, four years ago, I had never even heard of the word mysticism. The part he played in my conversion, by that book, was very great. From Gilson's *Spirit of Medieval Philosophy* I learned a healthy respect for Catholicism. Then *Ends and Means* taught me to respect mysticism. Maritain's *Art and Scholasticism* was another important influence, and Blake's poetry. Perhaps also Evelyn Underhill's *Mysticism*, though I read precious little of it. I was fascinated by the Jesuit sermons in Joyce's *A Portrait of the Artist as a Young Man*! What horrified him, began to appeal to me. It seemed to me quite sane. Finally G. F. Lahey's *Life of Gerard Manley Hopkins;* I was reading about Hopkins' conversion when I dropped the book and ran out of the house to look for Father Ford. All this reading covered a period of a year and a half or two years—during which I read almost all of Father Weiger's translations of Buddhist texts into French, without understanding them.

Years afterwards Merton was to read and interpret Buddhist texts with great understanding, and the mention of them at this early stage shows how the main trends in his life tended to reveal themselves early and to be long maturing. Blake, read and barely comprehended by a teen-age boy, helped in the conversion of a man ten years afterwards; Buddhist texts, read with an understandable lack of attention when the revelation of Christian truth was the burning urgency in Merton's mind, assisted him in a radical broadening of his mental and spiritual field of vision twenty years later.

One cannot say that Merton started writing while he was at Columbia; already in the Lycée at Montauban, he tells us in *The Seven Storey Mountain*, he and his friends were producing romantically adventurous novels in French. But at Columbia he first turned to writing as a possible vocation. He not only wrote in campus publications but also did book reviews for the *New York Times* and the *Herald Tribune,* wrote poems, and during his period at Cambridge and Columbia produced no less than four and a half novels. All but one are beyond our judgement, since he destroyed them before entering Gethsemani. The survivor, originally entitled *The Journal of My Escape from the Nazis,* he kept for many years until, before leaving for Asia in 1968, he brought it out of his files and arranged for its publication; it appeared posthumously in 1969, under the title of *My Argument with the Gestapo: A Macaronic Journal.*

Merton appropriately chose Gerard Manley Hopkins, whose conversion had in a sense triggered his own final decision to enter the Church, as the subject for his doctoral thesis at Columbia. But the thesis was never completed, since the urge to proceed beyond mere conversion into deeper areas of dedication became too pressing for Merton to continue along the customary academic path. Envisaging a teaching career, he had begun to conduct extension courses at Columbia. But his compelling need to be more than a lay member of the Catholic community, to express his conversion in some dramatic gesture of world-renunciation, made him anxious to immerse himself in one of the religious orders.

There were really two possibilities only, though others often haunted Merton's mind. One—which appealed immediately to his innate romanticism—was to become a Franciscan friar. St. Francis has always been a saint particularly sympathetic to the Anglo-Celtic mind, perhaps because of his joy in the natural world and its creatures. That joy linked him also with the Buddhists—lovers of all living beings—to whom Merton would later draw so close.

The other possibility was the Trappist movement, the Cistercian Order of the Strict Observance, the most austere offshoot of the Benedictine order. The Trappists are silent but also cenobitic; they form communities dedicated to contemplation, rather than collections of eremitic individuals—such as the Carthusians and the Camaldolese—who follow that course in solitude as well as silence.

It was, I believe, inevitable that Merton should choose and sustain the Cistercian pattern, but he did so only after much indecision. His poet's sense of closeness to the Franciscan tradition tempted him first towards the path of active dedication. He knew, from the example of St. Francis himself, that the Franciscan emphasis on works was not incompatible with interludes of eremitic contemplative life. And in the summer of 1940 he followed his inclinations so far as to make his approach to the Franciscans with a view to becoming a novice. He began active work at that time by teaching at St. Bonaventure's College, a Franciscan foundation at Olean in New York State.

But on the eve of entering the Franciscan novitiate, Merton was overcome with a sense of unworthiness because of the wildness and irreverance of his past life. The Franciscans listened patiently to him, and, with perhaps more understanding than he then realized, suggested that he might postpone entering the novitiate, for a period at least — perhaps indefinitely. Merton interpreted as lack of interest what was doubtless a realization by the Franciscans that his heart did not really lie with them, however much at this time his thoughts might do. He was mortified by this discouragement, but continued to believe in his vocation, and resolved to live as a religious even if he were not accepted as one. He carried out the observances to the extent of praying the Divine Office every day as if he were already a priest. To fulfill his need for self-abnegation by an appropriate form of service, he considered abandoning his teaching role to work in a settlement house founded by the White Russian refugee, Baroness Catherine de Hueck Doherty. He went there, to the slums of Harlem, on several occasions, thus receiving his first lessons in what American racial relations meant in actual human terms.

It is legitimate to speculate on what Merton's life might have been if he had followed the lay apostolate that was accepted by Catholics deeply concerned with the injustice of modern society, for he had a great deal temperamentally and even intellectually in common with people like Catherine de Hueck Doherty or Dorothy Day of the *Catholic Worker* (to which he eventually became a regular contributor) or Ammon Hennacy with his One-Man Revolution. A high contempt for the twentieth-century social

order (particularly in its American manifestation) and a deep
compassion for its victims were in Merton from the beginning,
and in his own way he too believed in a kind of one-man revolution.
But he believed also, as Huxley did, and as Gandhi did in a
different way, that this revolution must be a change of heart,
and that the change of heart could take place only through the
mystery of the contemplative's perfect communion with God. He
came to believe that mysticism was an actual power in the world,
and that if only a few saints achieved complete self-transcendence,
the world through their spiritual strength might even be physi-
cally saved from destruction.

Merton's growing inclination towards a contemplative as distinct from an active vocation reached a climax in the spring of
1941, when he made a retreat at the Trappist monastery of Gethsemani in Kentucky. He went there at the suggestion of Daniel
Walsh, but this was not his first contact with the Trappists, for
on his trip to Italy in 1933 he had visited their monastery of Tre
Fontane on the outskirts of Rome.

"I went in to the dark, austere old church, and liked it," he
records in *The Seven Storey Mountain*. "But I was scared to visit
the monastery. I thought the monks were too busy sitting in their
graves beating themselves with disciplines. So I walked up and
down in the silent afternoon, under the eucalyptus trees, and the
thought grew in me: 'I should like to become a Trappist monk.'

"There was little danger of my doing so, then. The thought
was only a daydream—and I suppose it is a dream that comes to
many men, even men who don't believe in anything. . . . I had no
idea what Trappist monks were, or what they did, except that
they kept silence. In fact, I also thought they lived in cells like
the Carthusians, all alone."

Whatever shallow impulse may have moved Merton that day
in 1933 became deep and real eight years later, when he was certain of his vocation to be a monk and a priest and was merely
seeking how most aptly to fulfill it. Once he reached Gethsemani,
there was no doubt in his mind. The setting was secluded and
beautiful—and at no time in his life did Merton despise the splendour of creation, which he saw always as a manifestation of God's
glory. The discipline at Gethsemani was a good deal more harsh

than exists in most monasteries today, for in the 1940s the Trappists still kept to the original seventeenth-century rule of the Cistercians of the Strict Observance, with its almost complete silence (though a kind of sign language was allowed), its stress on work and obedience, its elaborate liturgical practices (which were by no means soundless since they involved many hours of austere Gregorian chanting) and its minutely detailed timetables and sumptuary rules. But this was what, at the end of his youth, Merton needed far more than the easier and — in its own benign way — more worldly pattern of twentieth-century Franciscanism.

The sense of the monastery as a focus of spiritual power came strongly to him during his first days at Gethsemani, and on the 7th April he noted in his *Secular Journal:*

> This is the center of America. I had wondered what was holding the country together, what has been keeping the universe from cracking in pieces and falling apart. It is places like this monastery — not only this one: there must be others. . . .
>
> This is the only real city in America — and it is by itself, in the wilderness.
>
> It is an axle around which the whole country blindly turns, and knows nothing about it. Gethsemani holds the country together the way the underlying substrata of natural faith that goes with our whole being and can hardly be separated from it, keeps living on in a man who has 'lost his faith' — who no longer believes in Being and yet himself *is,* in spite of his crazy denial that He Who IS mercifully allowed him to *be.*
>
> What *right* have I to be here?

And a few days later, on Holy Saturday, the eve of his departure, he noted: "I desire only one thing : to love God. Those who love Him, keep His commandments. I only desire to do one thing: to follow His will. I pray that I am at least beginning to know what that may mean. Could it ever possibly mean that I might some day become a monk in this monastery?"

It meant precisely that. On the 10th December the same year, after months spent gathering the documents which the monastery punctiliously demanded (some of them from wartime England) and making his arrangements with the draft board, Thomas Merton entered the Abbey of Gethsemani as a postulant.

It was almost exactly the half-way point of his life. He was nearly twenty-seven, and he would remain a member of the community of Gethsemani for exactly twenty-seven years, since he died in 1968 on the 10th December, the anniversary of his entry into the monastery.

Compared with the first half of his life, the second half was remarkably lacking in external events. The Cistercians are an enclosed order who work within their own walls to sustain themselves in the contemplative life and who carry on no active works in the outside world. Neither the rule that he had accepted nor his own inclinations led Merton to return often to the outside world. Though in his final years he had to go into Louisville fairly often for medical treatment, he rarely travelled far from Gethsemani until in 1968 he set out on the Asian journey which was devoted to monastic concerns, its specific destination being the congress in Bangkok of representatives of Catholic monasteries in Asia.

But the external uneventfulness of his existence did not mean that Merton lived inactively or even entirely serenely. The life of the monks of Gethsemani may have been silent so far as verbal communication was concerned, but it was busy and full of distractions, which increased when new postulants began to flood in after the war's end and a monastery which contained seventy monks when Merton joined it grew to four times that number and threw out satellite communities; at the same time the community farms were mechanized, and money-making industries like cheese-making and the baking of fruit cake were extended, all to the detriment of solitude and simple living. Merton himself was attracted to the solitary eremitic life as the perfect setting for infused contemplation, and even before Gethsemani became so internally active, he was troubled by the thought that he might find his true place not in a cenobitic order but in one of the orders that stressed solitude, like the Carthusians. His superiors discouraged him, and Merton, who took his vow of obedience seriously, accepted their advice.

In 1947 he took the solemn vows that committed him to become a lifelong monk, and in 1949 he was ordained as a priest. Two years later he became Master of Scholastics, directing and counselling the monks who had chosen to become priests. After four years in that position, he began a decade as Master of Novices, a difficult role which involved not only introducing newcomers to the life of the monastery but also deciding which postulants seemed fitted for a life of reclusion and which should be sent away.

All this time the ideal of the solitary life attracted him, and within the monastery he urged that the Cistercian rule in fact allowed for the presence of hermits attached to monastic communities and that there were late mediaeval precedents, if not more recent ones. Finally, in 1965, when he ceased to be Master of Novices, he was allowed to appropriate as a hermitage a cottage that had been used for visitors on retreats, and there he lived in partial solitude, though he was expected to take his midday meal in the abbey refectory so that his links with the community could be sustained. It was probably a wise compromise, for though Merton needed a measure of reclusion for his writing and for his spiritual exercises, he was also at heart an amiable and gregarious man who during his monastic career discovered that, even if he loathed the world in the more corrupt sense of that ambivalent word, he loved mankind.

The other great threat to serenity, at least in the early years at Gethsemani, was the conflict which Merton saw arising between his two vocations, that of monk and that of writer. By the time he wrote *The Seven Storey Mountain* he had at least in part resolved it, for there are several references to the analogical relationship between the aesthetic and the contemplative function and at one point Merton actually claims that he "had always understood that art was contemplation, and that it involved the action of the highest faculties of man." Yet there is no doubt that when he turned to monasticism, writing seemed to him a temptation that might draw a veil between him and the truth. On the last page of *The Secular Journal,* written two weeks before he entered Gethsemani, there is a poignant cry from the heart. "Going to live in Harlem does not seem to me to be anything special. It is a good and reasonable way to follow Christ. But going to the Trappists is exciting, it fills me with awe and with desire. I return to the idea again and again: 'Give up *everything,* give up *everything!*'"

By *everything,* so emphasized, he meant most of all writing. But it was Gethsemani that did not allow him to give up writing and showed him that his two vocations were complementary rather than incompatible. He found himself impelled to write poems when he first reached the Abbey, and confessed it to his spiritual director, hoping that he would be forbidden to write and then would have to obey. But the confessor encouraged him to continue. He went to the Abbot, and to his surprise the Abbot not only added his own exhortations to continue but also suggested that Merton's writing might be used for the benefit of the monastery and the faith. Here again it seems that, like the Franciscans at an earlier stage in his life, Merton's Cistercian superiors were showing much wisdom, realizing that his life as a contemplative and his activities as a writer were likely to feed each other, to his benefit and also to that of the Order and the Church. They can hardly have foreseen how Merton's interests would take new and wider directions through his writing so that he would become a kind of social activist while remaining a monastic contemplative.

Once Merton had decided that writing was compatible with his contemplative vocation, ecclesiastical censorship tended to trouble him, especially the internal censorship in his own order. While accepting it nominally, he questioned such interference with his writing; there was a libertarian streak in his nature, and, while he did not directly disobey, he often found ways of manifesting his sense of freedom by evasion, as when he allowed his essays to be mimeographed and circulated privately, which in his view did not count as publication. From such practices, his letters suggest, he gained a good deal of sly amusement.

Sometimes his differences with the censors were on points of dogma; more frequently after the late 1950s, when Merton became involved from a distance in the civil rights movement and later denounced the war in Vietnam, the interference took on a quasi-political form, since Merton's statements were unpopular with many right-wing Catholics within and outside the hierarchy who believed that a monastic writer of such eminence could not speak without compromising the Church. However, after Vatican II the situation changed rapidly, and in the last few years of his life Merton was able to speak out as he wished in virtual freedom from ecclesiastical interference.

After his first five years in the monastery Merton began to

write copiously and in about twenty years he produced the sixty volumes published during his life and posthumously. (Large numbers of his articles and reviews published in periodicals of various kinds remain uncollected.) All this he did while taking full part, until 1965, in the monastic life of Gethsemani, while holding responsible and time-consuming offices, and without neglecting the contemplative life. But he had energy and self-discipline, and, since his reclusion saved him from the distractions to which writers living in cities are liable, he was able to make full use of whatever time he had to himself.

From the beginning, Merton developed as an all-round man of letters in the European continental tradition, willing to turn his hand to any task that seemed worthy or necessary without feeling that in some way his creativity would be diluted or defiled. As a student he had written reviews, fiction, poetry, and articles and reports in college newspapers. In the monastery his writings covered an equally wide field, ranging from poetry and autobiography through a moralistic critique of world affairs, to philosophy, theology, religious history, comparative religion and hagiography. He anthologized Gandhi and the Desert Fathers; he translated poems from French and Latin, Spanish and Portuguese; he was one of the most sensitive mediators between western traditions and the ways of thought and life represented by Taoism and Zen Buddhism.

Merton's writing — partly because of its great quantity — was by no means of even quality. He often wrote in haste, tending to rely on the corrective instincts of publishers' editors, and many of his books were compilations of periodical articles or extracts from journals. He seems to have deliberately favoured the tentative nature of this mosaic form, just as he was happiest writing concretely, with a good use of visual and auditory imagery, rather than writing in abstract terms, when he was often stiff and not always very clear. Early on, Daniel Walsh identified Merton as an Augustinian rather than a Thomist by nature; "he meant that my bent was not so much towards the intellectual, dialectical, speculative character of Thomism, as towards the spiritual, mystical, voluntaristic and practical way of St. Augustine and his followers." And, one might add, of William Blake. Certainly, at its best,

Merton's writing falls into the Augustinian-cum-Blakeian pattern, though in later years when he entered into social-moralistic controversy, he showed himself capable of very effective and sensible rational discourse.

At its worst, to be sure, his writing was very bad. His special kind of hackwork was not the periodical journalism to which writers in the outer world often have to resort but the books he wrote in his early Cistercian days for the benefit of the monastery and the Order. These included monastic histories and lives of Cistercian saints, and Merton himself in later years admitted that books like *What Are These Wounds?* — life of St. Lutgarde — and *Exile Ends in Glory* — the life of a particularly holy Trappist nun — were works to be ashamed of. Even in some of his better books, like *The Seven Storey Mountain,* there are passages of callow and shallow pietism which detract from the vigorous concreteness of the book in which they are set. *Seeds of Contemplation,* a series of meditations on meditation published originally in 1949, is an example of Merton's own maturing mind critically at work on his own writing, for, as we shall see later, by the time it reached a third and final version as *New Seeds of Contemplation* in 1961, its early dogmatic rigidities had been softened and its excesses of pietism tamed; in the process its appeal had been opened far beyond the narrowly Catholic readership for which it seemed originally intended.

It is Merton's writings that will, essentially, be the subject of the rest of this book — those events that mediate between the inward of the contemplative life and the outward of the world where books link us with other minds. Obviously in such a concise study as this it is impossible to discuss all of Merton's books in depth, and to mention them sketchily would be pointless, since they are all listed in the bibliography. As I have suggested, some are either too poor or too limited in their appeal to justify consideration here. From the rest, I shall select for attention as fairly as I can those which best illustrate the facets of Merton's thought and achievement to which I devote the following chapters.

2

Youth Between Wars

"I had never been able to write verse before I became a Catholic," says Thomas Merton in *The Seven Storey Mountain*. "I had tried, but I had never really succeeded, and it was impossible to keep alive enough ambition to go on trying." He tells how in November 1938 he "acquired a sudden facility for rough, raw Skeltonic verses" which lasted for a month, and that afterwards he "had many kinds of sounds ringing in my ears and they sometimes asked to get on paper."

Indeed, Merton's literary career, as far as he chose to preserve its results, dated entirely from his conversion. Writing in three different genres exists from this period between his baptism in 1938 and his admittance in December 1941 into the Abbey of Gethsemani, but none of it can be regarded as in any true sense the writing of a layman, since it was all done when he already wished to become a monk and a priest but did not yet realize where his vocation would lead him. In autobiography there is *The Secular Journal,* consisting of extracts from a diary written between October 1939 and November 1941 and ending shortly before he became a Trappist monk. There is his one surviving novel, *My Argument with the Gestapo,* and there are about forty poems, including those published posthumously in 1971 as *Early Poems.* Since we know that three and a half novels were destroyed, as well as a large portion of the diary from which *The Secular Journal* was extracted, it is obvious that these surviving texts were selected rather deliberately from a considerable mass of work which Merton produced during his years at Cambridge, Columbia and St. Bona venture's.

There is no great need to speculate on why these particular works were picked for preservation. Except for a few poems, all of them have some bearing on Merton's frame of mind at the time of his conversion and on his search for a vocation; they are, in their own way, documents of the religious life.

This is especially evident, despite its title, of *The Secular Journal*. In this case it is perhaps wise to interpret *secular* in its ecclesiastical sense of being within the Church yet also "in the world," as distinct from work of the period after 1941 when Merton retreated from the world by adopting a cenobitic rule. As he himself emphasizes in the preface he wrote for the journal's first publication, seventeen years after its last pages were written: "This is not the work of a monk or of a priest, but of a young layman recently converted to the Catholic faith and still struggling to find out whether or not he was supposed to dedicate his life to writing or to some higher and more special vocation. It is quite obviously not what one normally calls 'spiritual reading.' "

Yet, one might comment, the spiritual striving is always present, just as in Merton's monastic years the need to write was always there, and *The Secular Journal*'s appeal lies largely in the fact that it shows the dialectic interplay of these two urges in a less self-conscious way than they were later presented in *The Seven Storey Mountain,* that autobiography written with a very open eye for a pious Catholic readership.

The journal opens with an entry that reconciles the two Merton urges within a single image, for it is a discussion of Blake's idea that "all good poetry was poetry dictated by the angels," and it ends with a remark that seems to chart out not only the rest of Merton's existence as a layman but also the whole of his life on earth. "There is enough humility in poets from the moment they know that they are poets: because if they are, then they have to write in fear and trembling (as Blake told Samuel Palmer)." Fear and trembling are often enough evident in *The Secular Journal* as

Merton moves towards the moment of his symbolic abandonment of the world, but there is also a great deal of the joy of literature and of the arts in general, embodied in some of the most interesting critical comments that Merton made at any time.

He writes particularly acutely on Dante, defending the claim of the *Paradiso* rather than the *Inferno* to be considered the most impressive part of *The Divine Comedy*. He remarks that "It is easier to communicate a clear idea of the obscurity of hell than a clear idea of the clarity and brilliance of heaven," and one senses that his own longing for the beatific vision is guiding his judgement. Later—among comments on Marvell, Coleridge, Wordsworth—Merton talks with admiration and insight of Dylan Thomas. "His writing depends on a terrific coherence of sound and imagery overlying an incoherence, or maybe even lack of ideas. His poems are, then, kind of abstractions, but abstractions full of tremendous, sinewy craft and wit and inventiveness and vividness." And, remarking that Thomas, like many other modern poets, sets himself the task of walking through hell and describing everything objectively while remaining sane, he suggests his own divergent attitude by drawing the matter back to Dante. "Virgil pointed out all the damned to Dante, but covered the traveller's eyes for fear he should see the head of Medusa and turn to stone. Dylan Thomas and the others of this generation want to go through hell without Virgil, and hope they will not be turned to stone by Medusa. But they won't say they won't look, even at that terrifying spectacle."

In all this, one has the feeling that Merton had picked on Thomas's great weakness and also his great virtue; that despite his appearance of emotional raging, he was basically a superb poetic craftsman, writing in total sobriety—as he did—of the hell he experienced in intoxication. But the very superbness of the technique was an abstracting factor, and Merton's own sense of poetry lay in the opposite direction. There is a very significant passage in *The Secular Journal* where he contrasts "the logic of mathematics" which makes "a flight from the concrete into abstraction" with "the logic of the poet—that is, the logic of language and experience itself" which "develops the way a living organism grows." And an organic growth "is never ideal, only free. Never typical, always individual." The concrete and the organic, the free and the individual: in all the apparent inconsistencies of Merton's later writing and thinking, these are the Augustinian categories that endure.

Throughout *The Secular Journal* there are overt and implied references to the autonomy of truth, which exists in the realm of natural reason and does not need the Church's approval, and in anticipation of his later openness to other creeds and ways of thinking, Merton calls for writers merely to "tell the truth in their own terms. . . ." Such telling of the truth, he suggests when he is writing—as an artist's son—of painters and painting, can be its own mirror of the spiritual world, for "the intellectual grasp of some kind of perfection, which gives us pleasure when we look at a picture with our minds working, as well as our senses, gives us some basis for talking analogically of the joys of heaven."

At one point within *The Secular Journal,* Merton remarks that he is writing it because "I can't read novels any more," and a journal is "the kind of thing I like to do." The journal was, of course, to be a favourite form which he continued to use throughout his life, as examples like *The Sign of Jonas, Conjectures of a Guilty Bystander* and *The Asian Journal* demonstrate, and he used it well right from the beginning. *The Secular Journal,* like all the others, conveys both spontaneity and the sense of a controlling intelligence in its mosaic sequence of apparently disparate notes through which a progression and a form develop, enabling us to follow with great absorption these two crucial years of its author's life.

Interspersing literary notes with notes on spiritual searchings, the signals of his two vocations, the journal builds up through the last months of Merton's New York life to its first climax, which is a journey to Cuba where he joyfully shares the life of a fervently Catholic people (as Cubans seemed in 1940). Then, with his departure from New York to teach at St. Bonaventure's, it builds up again to the tensions of indecision before his departure to Gethsemani.

Merton himself thought the Cuban section of the journal was better than anything he had yet done in fiction, and indeed it is a piece of travel writing—an outer and an inner journey combined—in which Merton shows to the full his power to control concrete imagery, the whole rich detail of the visible world, in the service of a non-material end; his observation is clear and vivid, his power of empathizing with strange cultures is intense.

The high point of the Cuban interlude is the epiphany that Merton experiences in the church of San Francisco in Havana when a brown-robed friar is leading the children in song. He describes it with a clear simplicity lacking in some of his later, more elaborate and at times more cloying accounts of religious experiences.

> Before any head was raised again the clear cry of the brother in the brown robe cut through the silence with the words "Yo Creo..." "I believe" which immediately all the children took up after him with such loud and strong and clear voices, and such unanimity and such meaning and such fervor that something went off inside me like a thunderclap and without seeing anything or apprehending anything extraordinary through any of my senses (my eyes were open on only precisely what was there, the church), I knew with the most absolute and unquestionable certainty that before me, between me and the altar, somewhere in the center of the church, up in the air (or any other place because in no place), but directly before my eyes, or directly present to some apprehension or other of mine which was above that of the senses, was at the same time God in all His essence, all His power, all His glory, and God in Himself and God surrounded by the radiant faces of the uncountable thousands upon thousands of saints contemplating His glory and praising His Holy Name. And so the unshakable certainty, the clear and immediate knowledge that heaven was right in front of me, struck me like a thunderbolt and went through me like a flash of lightning and seemed to lift me clean up off the earth.
>
> To say that this was the experience of some kind of certainty is to place it as it were in the order of knowledge, but it was not just the apprehension of a reality, of a truth, but at the same time and equally a strong movement of delight, great delight, like a great shout of joy and in other words it was as much an experience of loving as of knowing something, and in it love and knowledge were completely inseparable. . . .

After his return from Cuba, Merton is concerned equally with the horrors of a war for which he feels in part guilty, and with the hesitations of his own spiritual course: the waitings, above all, for some sense of clear direction. He goes in the spring to Gethsemani, and everything about the monastery, from the work to the Gregorian singing, moves and fascinates him. Yet on his return he continues to write his journal with half a mind towards a career of teaching and writing, until, even in November, with Catherine de Hueck Doherty urging him to join her in Harlem, he is still telling himself to "make no decisions until the time for making decisions," though already by this time his inclinations were all towards becoming a Trappist, and the only real decision was when to cross the threshold of Gethsemani.

A good deal of the travails of this period enter, in lightly disguised form, into the curious book which was the only work of fiction Merton chose to preserve from his pre-monastic life, *My Argument with the Gestapo: A Macaronic Journal.* In *The Secular Journal* there are a few references to fiction — one of them to Graham Greene's *Brighton Rock,* which Merton admired greatly for the way it put the thriller form and "a kind of modified surrealism" into the service of what was essentially a parable. He also discusses James Joyce, first in relation to his lapsed Catholicism, and later in relation to the formal definition of his writings. Having decided that he now finds *Dubliners* unsatisfying, he remarks:

"Maybe the whole of *Dubliners,* especially 'The Dead,' is an indication of the fact that the novel as it has been established by the eighteenth century and perfected by the nineteenth is dead. *Ulysses* is a different kind of novel, a journal and a mobile, not a novel. *Finnegan's Wake* is a mobile. . . . *A Portrait of the Artist* is not a novel, but more of a journal."

Clearly these thoughts were in Merton's mind when, largely impelled by the news of the bombing of London and other English cities, he began — about the same time as he jotted these notes on Joyce and the fate of the novel — to write *The Journal of My Escape from the Nazis,* which eventually became *My Argument with the Gestapo: A Macaronic Journal.*

Unfortunately we know very little about Merton's earlier novels; he seems to have been thorough in destroying them without a trace. Naomi Burton, who was his literary agent in the 1940s, remembers two of them, both rather wild, at times funny, and somewhat autobiographical. They were called *The Man in the Sycamore Tree* and *The Labyrinth,* and Merton gave at least a sketch of the latter in *The Seven Storey Mountain.* It started off as *The Straits of Dover* and became *The Night Before the Battle* before it eventually metamorphosed, much shortened, into *The Labyrinth.*

> It was partly autobiographical, . . . but . . . I found the writing of it easier and more amusing if I mixed up a lot of imaginary characters in my own story. It is a pleasant way to write. When the truth got dull, I could create a diversion with a silly man called Terence Metrotone. I later changed him to Terence Park, after I showed the first draft of the book to my uncle, who abashed me by concluding that Terence Metrotone was a kind of acrostic for my-self. That was, as a matter of fact, very humiliating, because I had made such a fool of the character.

I suspect that *The Labyrinth* was rather in the manner of Evelyn Waugh, whom Merton read assiduously in England and whose Father Rothchild remained one of his favourite characters in fiction. *My Argument with the Gestapo,* though like the earlier and lost novels it contained a strong element of autobiography, had absorbed other and more portentous influences. Merton said in 1947 that "it was the kind of book I liked to write, full of double-talk and all kinds of fancy ideas that sounded like Franz Kafka," and in 1968 he described it as "a kind of sardonic medi-tation on the world in which I then found myself: an attempt to define its predicament and my own place in it. That definition was necessarily personal. I do not claim to have gained full access to the whole myth of Europe and the West, only to my own myth. But as a child of two wars, my myth had to include that of Europe and of its falling apart: not to mention America with its own built-in absurdities."

My Argument is in many ways best understood as a valedic-tory. It considers the falseness of the world between wars and says goodbye to the Thirties and their illusions. Merton himself, when he looked at the book in 1951, at a turning point in his monastic progress, was critical of its manner of dismissing the world; the pervading suggestion that the world is evil he regarded as a false solution, leading as it did to the idea that the world had "to be first ridiculed, then spat upon, and at last formally rejected with a curse." He commented that "I can do nothing whatever for my own salvation or for the glory of God if I merely withdraw from the mess people are in and make an exhibition of myself and write a big book saying, 'Look! I am different!'" And he went on to say that *My Argument* was "the result of a psychological withdrawal." (*The Sign of Jonas*)

One can agree that *My Argument* represents a psychological withdrawal if this is to be understood in the sense of saying goodbye not only to what Merton then conceived as worldly illusions but also to the self that was possessed by those illusions. *My Argument* seems to be the novel in which Merton actually took the least pains to disguise his autobiographical motivation. The main character is actually called Thomas Merton, his memories of England and France are identical with those of his creator, and at one especially Kafkaesque point a British intelligence officer reads out to him—and he acknowledges—the biographical details of the actual Merton.

One quickly becomes aware, however, that the aim of this book is not that of the ordinary autobiographical novel, which is usually an exercise in ego-enhancement. Merton is projecting his past, historic self onto a fictional character in order to abandon him, and thus *My Argument* takes its place in the process of self-abnegation in which its author was actively engaged at this time and which led to his temporary metamorphosis into Brother Louis, the Trappist monk.

The plot is that of return to the site of a past life. Merton actually left England in 1934, and he did not go back in the years before his retreat into the Abbey of Gethsemani. But in *My Argument* he imagines himself returning, and this journey of the mind lends itself to a kind of surrealistic treatment. Merton describes the book as a journal, and this description has to be taken on two levels. It is the diary of the imagined journey, and it is also allowed to expand to include passages of reminiscence as well as dreams which are only a little less fantastic than what appears to be taking place in the waking world, so that an atmosphere of transfigured reality envelops the whole book.

The reminiscences are all of events which took place in Merton's own life, and which he treated a little more literally shortly afterwards when he described them in the direct autobiography of *The Seven Storey Mountain*. But we are also aware, as we follow the fictional Merton through the tumbling ruins of falling London and over to France where he goes through some mild adventures with the Gestapo, that we are watching a symbolic presentation of the author's inner predicament at the time of writing the book, and that the motivation behind the novel was much less "a sense of identification, by guilt, with what was going on in England," than a desire to externalize the problems of the quest that at St. Bonaventure's in the summer of 1941 left him undecided about the real nature of his spiritual vocation. This is the second level of the journal.

The Merton of the novel has been in London for only a few hours when his journal begins. He establishes contact with a number of people he knew in the past, including a childhood sweetheart and a tweedy, doggy Mrs. Frobisher whose counterpart certainly existed in the author's real English youth. From Mrs. Frobisher he passes on to the mysterious Madame Gongora, a citizen of the neutral and non-existent country of Casa, from which Merton himself, as it turns out, has a forged passport. After an escapade in the country with Madame Gongora, when they take the wrong road and find themselves in a secret military site, Merton is dogged by detectives and eventually interrogated by British intelligence officers who then connive at his going to France on a vague clandestine mission which leads him to Paris. There the Gestapo investigate him and eventually dismiss him as a harmless eccentric with a taste for writing pornographic memoirs. The book ends with Merton sending the manuscript of his journal to America in the care of a departing foreign correspondent. He is left in his room in the captive city, about to begin a new journal.

"I think suddenly of Blake, filling paper with words, so that the words flew about the room for the angels to read, and after that, what if the paper was lost or destroyed?

"That is the only reason for wanting to write, Blake's reason."

On the face of it, *My Argument with the Gestapo* might seem to be a belated successor to the semi-surrealistic myth-oriented fictions that figured so considerably in the writing of the Thirties, taking dramatic form in plays like the Auden-Isherwood *Ascent of F. 6* and *The Dog Beneath the Skin* and novelistic form in the books of Rex Warner and Graham Greene. All these fictions, whether they were meant to be acted or read, were also intended to be considered parables. Their stylized improbabilities, their dreamlike actions, were conditioned in part by the current interest in the mythology of Sir James Frazer and the dream psychology of Freud and Jung, but also in part by the didactic intentions characteristic of the writing of the period — even including the religiously oriented plays and poems that T. S. Eliot was then writing. The left-wing writers, with decreasing enthusiasm, projected their Communist-tinged radicalism; the Catholic writers such as Graham Greene presented the drama of religious faith in an irreligious world and the paradoxical co-existence of belief and sin, of knowledge and damnation.

By relating *My Argument* to the writings of Kafka, Merton in fact takes us a little farther than the didacticism of the Thirties, which in his mind was already somewhat discredited. Years later, in *The Sign of Jonas*, he would confess to the fascination which Kafka, like Rilke, had for him as a different kind of solitary being, and in *My Argument* he — like Kafka — takes us into the world and the predicament of the assailed yet lonely soul. There are, of course, other influences evident in *My Argument*. The English characters and even Madame Gongora and her sinister major-domo, Valdes, are of the same breed as the inhabitants of Evelyn Waugh's satirical novels of English life between the wars, and the macaronic dialogue which at times shatters with bursts of sheer extravagance the general simplicity of the style betrays the lingering influence of Joyce and especially of *Finnegan's Wake*. The descriptions of crumbling London have a Greeneish tone. But the presentation of a character on a quest whose aim he does not fully know, and subject to the pressures of forces he does not understand, brings *My Argument* very close to Kafka, in more than mere literary strategy. For, just as Kafka used his writing to externalize his inner spiritual drama, so Merton used *My Argument* at least in part to work his way through his own doubts and difficulties at this crucial time of decision. And this, I suggest, is why he did not destroy this alone of his novels, and why he wished it to be published long after he had abandoned any ambitions to succeed as a novelist. In other words, he did not regard it as a novel in the ordinary sense of the word, since at the deepest level it was not fictional; it was, as he called it, a journal — the most veiled and indirect of all his journals.

It is clear that the "sense of identification, by guilt, with what was going on in England" represented only the shallowest level of intention in *My Argument*. Merton is indeed appalled at the war, and he recognizes his own guilt, as he recognizes the guilt of every other Christian, since it seems to him their spiritual inadequacies are responsible for the very existence of the conflict. But he identifies himself with no side, and much of the novel is taken up with a parodic mockery of the propaganda images which both the British and the Germans were seeking to project of themselves through such media as film, radio and the press; it is clear that returning to France, even to a captured and humiliated Paris, is to plunge into a way of life more morally and spiritually authentic, just because it has withdrawn from the fray, than that of the rest of Europe.

It is really as the mysterious quest for a never-defined personal goal that *My Argument* takes on its deepest and most tantalizing significance. Merton represents himself as "trying to find something, I know not what." Challenged with, "You are an exile, stranger!" he answers, "Yes, I am an exile all over the earth." Questioned about his dubious papers, he replies, "I will wear any label you hitch upon my collar, in the world's wide prison. But though you give me a license that says I am a social animal, I continue to know that I am a child of God." And later in the same Kafkaesque interview with the two officers the fictional Merton makes a statement in which we feel the real Merton is crying from the heart:

> But if you want to identify me, ask me not where I live, or what I like to eat, or how I comb my hair, but ask me what I think I am living for, in detail, and ask me what I think is keeping me from living fully for the thing I want to live for. Between these two answers you can determine the identity of any person. The better answer he has, the more of a person he is.

. . . I am all the time trying to make out the answer, as I go on living. I live out the answer to my two questions myself and the answer may not be complete, even when my life is ended: I may go on working out the answer for a long time after my death, but at last it will be resolved, and there will be no further question, for with God's mercy I shall possess not only the answer but the reality that the answer was about.

All this is reinforced by clues that link the preoccupations of Merton in Europe with those of the actual Merton at that time in America: references to the Trappists, to mystics like St. John of the Cross and Jakob Boehme, to theologians like Karl Barth. The Hotel Rocamadour, in which the fictional Merton stays in Paris, is named after a famous shrine to the Virgin Mary which impressed Merton when he visited it with his father as a child, while Madame Gongora shares her name with the great Spanish poet Luis de Góngora y Argote, like Merton in this novel a writer much addicted to word-play and very significantly the author of a notable poetic cycle, his best work, known as the *Soledades,* the Solitudes; one wonders whether there is not in fact some link between the mysterious Madame Gongora and La Soledad, Our Lady of Solitude, whose "little dressed-up image" Merton found in a church in Cuba, remarking in memory that she was "one of his big devotions." (*The Seven Storey Mountain*) Her country of Casa, which means "house" and to which the fictional Merton has a passport, may be an allusion to the monastery, or religious house, which the real Merton thinks of entering and whose full title was the Abbey of Our Lady of Gethsemani.

Perhaps the way the book ends is a final clue. It is not a very definite or climactic ending. As Merton remarked in 1951, the book has no real progress. "A situation presents itself and the stream of the book — which after all has a stream — stops and forms a lake." The lake is the situation in France, out of which neither the fictional Merton nor his namesake who writes the novel has any clear idea of how to emerge. Such a stasis of course parallels Merton's condition of vocational indecisiveness at this time. And so the clue the ending gives is itself an indecisive one. Wrapping up his journal, sending it off to America "in the hands of a maniac who believes he understands world affairs, political rights and wrongs, and what is going to happen in the war" — these actions seem to signify the ending of a life. The pile of "new paper, white untouched" seems to suggest the *tabula rasa* which Merton hopes his new life will be once he abandons the past and retreats from the world.

The poems Merton wrote during this period are not among his best, but they deepen in various ways the impressions of inner experience that we gather from *The Secular Journal* and *My Argument with the Gestapo*. They include six poems dated 1939 which appear in the "Uncollected Poems" section of the *Collected Poems;* the sixteen poems of the volume *Early Poems,* published in 1971, and, according to Merton, about half the *Thirty Poems* which formed his first published book in 1944.

Though there are points when the resonance is true and sure, these poems are for the most part works of a young man who has not yet found a personal voice and who is not yet quite sure what to say when that voice begins to speak. They show with little disguise the influences to which at this time he was subject. The 1939 pieces include, for example, a graceful and appropriately Marvellian "Aubade: Bermuda":

> Now at our island's shining rim
> The waves upon their purpose run
> Each one busy to consult
> The mild opinions of the sun.

Other poems of the same time, which reflect Merton's disgust with the world as he now sees it, have a Skeltonesque satirical roughness, as in "Bureaucrats: Diggers":

> And oh, the mole crops tenderest shoots
> And tells the time by twisted roots.
> Some pismire's busy brain
> Conceived the subway train.

The same unsureness of identity is carried over into the *Early Poems,* which are evidently those Merton himself rejected in 1944 when he put his first book together. Most of them are neither fluent nor passionate, and one has the feeling of an assured prose writer — as *The Secular Journal* shows Merton to have been already—finding his way among the rhythms and images of an unfamiliar way of expression. Broad but unassimilated reading is suggested by the variety of manners he consciously or unconsciously parodies (there is an oddly Housmanesque little elegy called "Two British Airmen," and a rather sophomoric extravaganza which puts the story of the Athenian tribute of maidens to the minotaur into the form of an epithalamium entitled "from The Second Chapter of a Verse History of the World").

In many of these poems war and cities appear as manifestations of the disorder of the world. One of the best war pieces, entitled merely "Poem," begins with the kind of arresting cluster of sharp visual images that will later characterize Merton's poetry at its best:

> Light plays like a radio in the iron tree;
> Green farms fear the night behind me
> Where lightnings race across the western world.

and ends effectively with the flat despair of:

> The woman I saw fleeing through the bended wheat:
> I know I'll find her dead.

In tone and temper alike his city poems tend to echo Blake's perception of the evil and pathos of London, transferred in "Dirge for the City of Miami" to a place in modern America:

> Never did the drunkard think
> To taste such bitterness in his drink
> And there the gentle murderer stands,
> And sadly, sadly wipes his hands:
> There the forger and the thief
> And the bank robber bow in grief
> While up and down the perjurer goes,
> Picking his nose, picking his nose.

Apart from "The Tower of Babel," in which Merton anticipated the morality play he wrote under the same title in the 1950s by showing the malign power of words as distinct from "The Word," the most significant of the *Early Poems* are the two final fragments, in which he records his decision to enter Gethsemani, and does so with a simple power that shows the sudden coalescence

of true words and true feeling. In "Lent (A Fragment)" he celebrates the entry into silence:

> Close, eyes, and soul, come home!
> Senses will seem to perish, in the desert:
> Thought will pretend to live on punishment, among the empty
>   tombs.

> 'Til pride, amid the rocks and sepulchers of Thebes, lies quiet.

and in "Sacred Heart 2 (A Fragment—)" he anticipates the end of
wandering:

> Geography comes to an end,
> Compass has lost all earthly north,
> Horizons have no meaning
> Nor roads an explanation. . . .

It is not entirely easy to isolate those of the *Thirty Poems*
which were actually written before Gethsemani. One of them,
and in my view one of the best of Merton's early poems, is certainly "Song from Our Lady of Cobre," which he wrote in Cuba:

> The white girls lift their heads like trees,
> The black girls go
> Reflected like flamingoes in the street.
> The white girls sing as shrill as water,
> The black girls talk as quiet as clay.

> The white girls open their arms like clouds,
> The black girls close their eyes like wings:
> Angels bow down like bells,
> Angels look up like toys,

> Because the heavenly stars
> Stand in a ring:
> And all the pieces of the mosaic, earth,
> Get up and fly away like birds.

Here, in a quite fragile lyric, the virtues one sees in Merton's better
later poems are brought together for the first time: concreteness
and a sharp originality of imagery; a sensitive counterpointing of
words (monosyllables in relation to polysyllables); a quiet, sure

rhythm; devotion evident but all the more poignant for being indirectly stated; vision without pietism.

Other poems in this collection which appear to have been written before Gethsemani restate themes of political disaster, as in "The Night Train," and contrast the beauty of God's creation, and the innocence with which children perceive it, with the corrupted vision of those who seek to mar it because their lives have been marred by the loss of spiritual direction:

> And when their shining voices, clean as summer,
> Play, like churchbells over the field,
> A hundred dusty Luthers rise from the dead, unheeding,
> Search the horizon for the gap-toothed grin of factories,
> And grope, in the green wheat,
> Toward the wood winds of the western freight.
>
>   ("Aubade: Lake Erie") '

The best of the poems which I believe date from the pre-monastic days are, in my view, "Iphigenia: Politics" and "In Memory of the Spanish Poet Federico García Lorca." "Iphigenia" is one of a number of poems Merton wrote at this period, using the myths of classical antiquity to make statements about the world of his time. Iphigenia, the daughter of Agamemnon sacrificed to ensure a victory, becomes the truth which politicians kill, in this way creating a future holding terrors as fearful as the vengeance that finally awaited Agamemnon:

> This is the way the ministers have killed the truth, our daughter,
> Steps lead back into the rooms we fear to enter;
> Our minds are bleaker than the hall of mirrors:
>
> And the world has become a museum.

Iphigenia is a sacrificial figure, but Lorca, in whom so many poets of all nations and political views have seen an image of the life of the imagination destroyed by mental darkness, becomes for Merton a Christ-like martyr of the modern world. The guitars of Spain, the poem tells us, have never forgotten Lorca's name, and the woman who sings, her voice "turned to iron in the naked air,/ More loud and more despairing than a ruined tower," seems to project the vast human tragedies that his death portended. The poem ends in the refrain:

> (Under what crossless Calvary lie your lost bones, Garcia Lorca?
> What white Sierra hid your murder in a rocky valley?)

Behind the walls of Gethsemani Merton was to remain faithful to the poetry he shared with Lorca, and in all his turning from the world he would not finally forget that it was outside the Garden of the Agony, at the end of the world's dusty roads, that Christ's crucifixion took place.

3

The Walls of Gethsemani

"It is possible to doubt whether I have become a monk (a doubt I have to live with)," said Thomas Merton in 1961, "but it is not possible to doubt that I am a writer, that I was born one and will probably die as one." The occasion was certainly appropriate for such reflections, since Merton was writing the author's preface to *The Thomas Merton Reader,* a publication that not only set a seal on his literary standing, making it no longer possible to consider him other than a writer by vocation and perhaps even by profession, but also demonstrated rather dramatically that in one of the aims with which he had entered the Abbey of Gethsemani he had failed, and failed through being the person he was. He had gone into the monastery to lose himself to the world, and for many years of his journals we witness the curious and apparently contradictory situation of the obedient monk Brother Louis seeking to shed his worldly self known as Thomas Merton, while the same Thomas Merton in the world outside becomes a familiar and in some ways a symbolic figure in the eyes of a wide reading public.

Thomas Merton the artist in fact remained very much alive even when Thomas Merton the layman was theoretically dead, and Merton himself was constantly aware of the apparent dichotomy between his aims as a monk and as a writer. This awareness perhaps explains why, unlike his fellow poet William Everson, who became a Dominican friar and then both lived and wrote under his religious name of Brother Antoninus, Merton kept one name for the monastery and another for the public. Father Louis never published a line under his monastic name; Thomas Merton never performed a sacerdotal act.

One of the wisdoms Merton in fact learned by the end of his first monastic decade was that, as Emerson put it, "a foolish consistency is the hobgoblin of little minds." He recognized that his inner self had many facets of expression, and that the aesthetic and the mystical impulses, which he always recognized as possessing an analogical relationship, were equally strong and durable within him. In the same way he balanced his desire for solitude, that longing which in his novice days made him think of entering the severest order of eremites he could discover, with his strong inclination towards the brotherhood in Christ which the cenobitic life offered him, and in 1958, at a time when he was also becoming reconciled to the inevitability of remaining a writer to the end, he remarked, in *Notes on Solitude:* "Do not flee to solitude from the community. Find God first in the community, then he will lead you to solitude."

In all the turmoil of mind that attended this apparent confusion of directions, one cannot help seeing Merton as a man more blessed than most of his fellows, for in the ways that mattered most his deepest desires were fulfilled. He became a good, a successful, an influential writer. He finally achieved his hermitage within the community and in the meantime he had learned that solitude is not a matter of place. And to the end he remained a good and conscientious monk, punctiliously following the most difficult rule of all—that of obedience—and, as his Benedictine friend Jean Leclercq once said, seeing "everything through a monk's eye." All those who associated with him in the monastery, and later wrote of him in Patrick Hart's collection of reminiscences, *Thomas Merton: Monk,* testify to his humility and dedication, and one can perhaps no better define the drift of Merton's whole way of thought and writing, including his way of poetry, than by his own statement, made on his last journey, about the marginality of the monk—and the poet as well—in the modern technocratically dominated world. "He struggles with the fact of death, trying to seek something deeper than death, and the office of the monk, or the marginal person, the meditative person or the poet, is to go beyond death even in this life, to go beyond the dichotomy of life and death and to be, therefore, a witness to life."

In the intimate journals which Merton wrote throughout his monastic life and in his poems, even more than in his didactic and quasi-theological writings, one finds the witness to life, as against the rejection of the world, constantly exemplified, and there is no doubt that the monastery entered deeply into his writing both as an experience and as an unexpectedly liberating factor. Merton would have probably continued as a writer even if he had never vanished behind the walls of Gethsemani, but there is nothing to suggest that he would have turned out to be much more than a worthy academic scholar, writing good poetry and criticism in his spare time and perhaps in the end producing some fiction that the publishers might have found more acceptable than his apprentice works. The promise is there in the early writings, but it does not strike one as an exceptional promise. It was his religious life that gave Merton the special experience and the inner dynamic that forced him to keep on writing, and also provided the creatively inhibiting circumstances — lack of time and privacy and a censorious conscience — that narrowed the impulse like a jet of water and heightened the intensity.

Of Merton's many poems about his monastic vocation one of the best was a comparatively early piece, "The Quickening of St. John the Baptist: On the Contemplative Vocation," which appeared in his third volume, *Figures for an Apocalypse* (1947). Merton envisages the unborn John awakening in Elizabeth's womb when he hears the voice of the Virgin Mary as she enters the house. And he continues:

> You need no eloquence, wild bairn,
> Exulting in your hermitage.
> Your ecstasy is your apostolate,
> For whom to kick is *contemplata tradere.*
> Your joy is the vocation
> Of Mother Church's hidden children —
> Those who by vow lie buried in the cloister or the hermitage:

The speechless Trappist, or the grey, granite Carthusian,
The quiet Carmelite, the barefoot Clare,
Planted in the night of contemplation,
Sealed in the dark and waiting to be born.

Night is our diocese and silence is our ministry
Poverty our charity and helplessness our tongue-tied sermon.
Beyond the scope of sight or sound we dwell upon the air
Seeking the world's gain in an unthinkable experience.
We are exiles in the far end of solitude, living as listeners
With hearts attending to the skies we cannot understand:
Waiting upon the first far drums of Christ the Conqueror,
Planted like sentinels upon the world's frontier.

The life of contemplatives at "the far end of solitude" in the kind of monastery that Merton entered in 1941 was a severe and arduous one. The order he entered, the Cistercians of the Strict Observance, more generally known as the Trappists, had a traditional reputation for the rigours of its rule. Though there are in fact severer orders in Europe, it was nevertheless a dramatic shift from Merton's life as a lay teacher in a Franciscan college, even though he tried to live a life modelled on that of a priest, to his subjection to a rule of life more rigorous than that of many jails and to a pattern of constant prayer, and work as prayer, that any man not dedicated to self-transformation at any cost would have found an intolerable incarceration in itself.

The history of the Cistercian Order is one of successive rigorist reforms within the monastic movement. The Benedictines, the principal contemplative order of the early middle ages, had been paradoxically corrupted by the piety of mediaeval laymen who liberally donated and willed money and land to the monasteries. Monasteries then became not only prosperous landlords but also powerful forces in a worldly sense within the feudal order. In England, for example, the leading Benedictine monks—the mitred abbots—ranked with the bishops as peers of the realm and sometimes took civil office in the king's administration. In such circumstances, observances became lax, luxuries found their way into the Benedictine abbeys; the stage was set for the appearance of the sybaritic monks who would arouse the just mockery of

Chaucer and Langland and become favourite victims in many a representation of the Dance of Death.

It was inevitable that the more dedicated monks should desire a return to the strictness of early Benedictine life, with a renewed emphasis on the contemplative path, and in 1098 — in one of the many internal reformations that preceded the schismatic movements of the sixteenth century which we now call *the* Reformation — St. Robert of Molesmes led a breakaway group from his monastery to set up a new foundation near Dijon at Cîteaux, from which the Cistercian Order takes its name. St. Stephen Harding, a close successor of St. Robert, elaborated the rule that distinguished the Cistercians from the unreformed Benedictines. All feudal revenues were rejected, and the monks were expected to provide for themselves by manual labour; severe asceticism was accompanied by a simplification of the liturgy and of ecclesiastical ornamentation. All Cistercian monasteries were to follow the same uniform rule, and this was to be assured by annual general chapters at Cîteaux, where the abbots of all the houses would gather, and by periodical visitations to the daughter houses by the heads of the founding abbeys. Individual monks were expected to stay all their lives in the monasteries where they began as novices.

The twelfth century, when St. Bernard founded the famous abbey of Clairvaux, became a period of extraordinary expansion for the Cistercians. In his own way, Bernard, "the Mellifluous Doctor," was an extremely effective missionary, and under his inspiration no less than 68 daughter houses were founded from Clairvaux alone. By St. Bernard's death in 1153, the Cistercian order had spread across all of Catholic Europe and claimed almost four hundred monasteries.

The Cistercians suffered the same penalty of success as the Benedictines before them. The proliferation of monasteries made it difficult to continue effectively the visitations and general chapters by which St. Stephen Harding had sought to sustain uniformity and austerity. Abbeys once again acquired possessions in return for prayerful intercessions on behalf of their benefactors, and in proportion as they became wealthy the discipline slackened. Popes and kings interfered in the elections of abbots at the wealthier monasteries, sometimes imposing clerics who were not even members of the order but who had political influence.

When the Reformation came, the Cistercians were condemned along with the other orders, and in northern Europe nobody stood up to defend them. Their function seemed to have become irrelevant in a world where chiliasts of all kinds moved among the people.

In the rest of Europe they were also weakened when the counter-Reformation, that dramatic afterthought of active minds in a Church half-dead from institutional schlerosis, tended to place an emphasis on the activist orders in contrast to the contemplatives. The Church seemed to need teachers and preachers, and the initiative moved to orders such as the Jesuits and the Dominicans, while the enclosed orders rapidly lost, in the new world of the Renaissance, the special place which they had kept within feudal and pre-Reformation society. To many contemplative monks, the only way to ensure that their traditions survived seemed to be yet another internal reformation, another return to rigour and discipline. During the seventeenth century a number of attempts in this direction were made, and the most celebrated and successful was the new rule established by Armand-Jean Le Bouthillier de Rancé at his abbey of La Trappe. Manual labour, constant prayer, seclusion from the world and silence within the monastery were the foundations of the renewed rule. La Trappe and other reformed monasteries broke away to establish the Cistercian Order of the Strict Observance (the Trappists) with its own pattern of general chapters and visitations and of uniform observances.

The Abbey of Our Lady of Gethsemani, where Merton became a monk, had been founded in 1848 by French monks in the hills of Kentucky; the region was then remote from human habitation, and even in Merton's day the monastery's seven hundred acres of fields and woods bordered on wild forest land. Migration to the New World had done very little to change the monastic way of life, and when Merton became a postulant in 1941 and shortly afterwards a novice, the Trappist rule was observed in all its rigour, even though most of the monks were now American.

Like every other novice, Merton had to accept the rules of obedience, poverty, chastity, conversion of manners and stability, whose adoption he later confirmed by solemn vows. Throughout his twenty-seven years at Gethsemani he strove to fulfill these promises. The vow of poverty meant that every dollar he earned by writing went to the monastery and helped to subsidize the modernization and mechanization which it underwent during the later 1950s and the 1960s, a process which Merton personally regarded with great misgiving. There is nothing on record to suggest that the vow of chastity troubled him, and he lightly transgressed the vow of obedience only on the few occasions when he found ways of evading the rulings of ecclesiastical censors outside the monastery who had condemned his works. As for stability, he rarely went outside the walls of Gethsemani during his twenty-seven years there until he started on his great Asian journey, and even then, though he departed with the thought in his mind that he might find some place of retreat where he could be protected from the consequences of his own fame, he was soon looking forward to returning to his own abbey. It had indeed become in a very personal way his home, the place with which the world identified him but also the place where—a natural solitary—he could at last find acceptance on his own terms among the men who formed the most stable family he ever had, the intermittencies of his earlier days having made it difficult for him to attain intimate relationships with individuals. Though, as a good Catholic, Merton praised the married state, there is no sign that at any point in his life he ever considered so intimate a personal relationship a possibility for himself; the formalized brotherhood of the Trappist order, supplemented by many tenuous contacts through correspondence and occasional visits with people outside Gethsemani, provided as much as he temperamentally needed in human contacts through which to exercise his Christian love of other men. The well-authenticated tales of Merton in his later years hiding in the Kentucky woods to avoid visitors and intrusive retreatants reflect not merely a philosophic urge towards the solitude necessary for contemplation but also a natural shyness that made an excess of human company, and particularly of the company of celebrity-seekers, painful to him.

The rule of the conversion of manners—the most difficult for many postulants in its radical reorientation of even daily life on the basis of spiritual instead of material goods—was that which Merton accepted with the greatest enthusiasm, for with all its vigorous disciplines it meant the cessation of a secular life that had grown increasingly painful in its uncertainties. Here, at least in an exterior way, all was certain and predictable; remembering that time many years afterwards, Merton remarked: "Those were hard years, before the days when radiators were much in favor during the winter, when the hours of communal prayer were much longer, when the fasts were much stricter. It was a period of training, and a happy, austere one."

The Trappist regimen required the monks to rise at two in the morning. There followed two hours of prayers, which included the choral singing of Psalms, and of meditation. The hours of darkness, which can be symbolically related to that luminous darkness where according to the mystics God visits the harrowed soul, were considered of special importance, and after the Mass was celebrated at 4 a.m., there were more Psalms and prayers, followed by a reading period. The first meal came at 7 a.m. and it reflected the austerity of the diet, consisting of bread and coffee. The midday lunch, main meal of the day, consisted usually of bread and cooked vegetables, milk and cheese; meat, fish and eggs were served only in the infirmary to sick monks. In the evening there would be another light repast of bread and coffee with fruit or cheese, and at seven most of the monks would be in the cubicles of their dormitories, trying to sleep on the straw pallets laid on their beds of boards. They were expected to sleep in their full and heavy woollen habits even in the high summers, which at Gethsemani were exceptionally torrid; each monk had only a single change of habit, which meant a great deal of washing during the hot weather, and the discomfort was increased by the retention of cumbersome mediaeval types of underwear which the Cistercians had used since their foundation. Even this austere and anachronistic rule was intensified on certain days and seasons; during Lent there was no breakfast except in the infirmary, and the monks had to work hungry until noon; every Friday there were penitential sessions, with self-flagellation.

Apart from interludes of prayer and choral singing at the day Hours, the period between breakfast and retiring at 7 p.m. was taken up with whatever manual or intellectual work might be assigned by superiors, either in the abbey or on the monastery farm. Merton once estimated that his very considerable mass of writing was produced in the scanty two hours of actual leisure that a monk could extract from each day. At the time of Merton's apprenticeship in Gethsemani the rules of enclosure were strictly kept: monks had to remain within the cloisters unless they were assigned to work in the fields or woods. Though poor health often made such outside toil very painful for him, Merton always welcomed it. "How necessary it is," he says in *The Sign of Jonas,* "for monks to work in the fields, in the rain, in the sun, in the mud, in the clay, in the wind: these are our spiritual directors and our novice-masters. They form our contemplation. They instill us with virtue. They make us as stable as the land we live in. You do not get that out of a typewriter." And he ends with a quotation from the Rule of St. Benedict: "Those are in truth monks who live by the work of their hands as our Fathers and the Apostles did."

Merton gained pleasure as well as lessons in virtue out of escaping from the enclosure, and there are many passages in which he talks with a rather lush eloquence of absorbing the beauty of God's creation in a mood that is almost one of pantheistic ecstasy.

> But my chief joy is to escape to the attic of the garden house and the little broken window that looks out over the valley. There in the silence I love the green grass. The tortured gestures of the apple trees have become part of my prayer. I look at the shining water under the willows and listen to the sweet songs of all the living things that are in our woods and fields. So much do I love this solitude that when I walk out along the road to the old barns that stand alone, far from the new buildings, delight begins to overpower me from head to foot and peace smiles even in the marrow of my bones. (*The Sign of Jonas*)

Part of the rule of the conversion of manners was of course the famous Trappist rule of silence about which there have been many misconceptions among non-monastics. Contrary to the general impression, Trappists do not move around in a completely soundless world; that would be impossible in a well-populated monastery given to manual work and industry, and Merton's journals are studded with complaints of the degree of non-human noise that was made especially by the lay brothers, who appear to have wielded their mechanical tools with a zest that perhaps compensated for their inability to speak to each other. Once, visiting a Carmelite house in Louisville, Merton remarked on the contrast between this place, where people moved in slippered quiet, and the Trappist monastery, where the passages resounded with the clump of farm boots; the Carmelites extended their silence beyond speech.

But not even all speech was prohibited at Gethsemani. Conversation, regarded as distracting from the monastery's contemplative goal, was forbidden, and for transmitting necessary information a quite adequate sign language was developed which some of the more ingenious monks elaborated into a substitute for spoken conversation. Yet the vocal cords of the monks went by no means unused, nor was the natural desire to hear a human voice unsatisfied. Those who belonged to the choir — more than half the monks — chanted for hours every day; all the monks joined in vocal prayer; instruction was given to the scholastics and the novices in oral form; speech was allowed when the community met in chapter to discuss its affairs, and at every meal a monk would be chosen to read passages from some religious book aloud to those who were eating in the refectory. The rule in practice was that speech, abandoned for profane purposes, could still be used for sacred purposes, in the liturgy or in instruction. And, Merton argued in his introduction to *Silence in Heaven,* there is a close connection between such use of speech and silence itself:

> The monastic life is a life wholly centered upon this tremendous existential silence of God which nobody has ever been able to explain, and which is, nevertheless, the heart of all that is real. Other lives are dedicated to partial ends — to ends that can be verified and measured in terms of language, recorded, somehow, if not in physical sound, at least in a thought that sounds in the mind and is ready to reproduce itself and communicate its echoes to other men. The monastic life is not dedicated to a sounding communication among men. It lives by a soundless communication

in mystery between man and God, between man and his brother, and between man and all created things.

The value of the monks' Public Prayer is therefore not drawn so much from its sound as from the deep silence of God which enters into that sound and gives it actuality, value, meaning. The beauty of Gregorian chant, and that which distinguishes it from every other kind of music, lies in the fact that its measured sound, in itself beautiful, tends to lead the soul, by its beauty, into the infinitely more beautiful silence of God. Chant that does not have this effect, no matter how great its technical perfection, is practically without value. It is empty of the silence of wisdom, which is its substance and its life.

Merton himself had as many opportunities for speech as he desired. For fourteen years his responsibilities first as Master of Scholastics and then as Master of Novices included delivering lectures on theology and on monastic traditions. Also, as Master of Novices, he acted as spiritual director to those under his charge, conversing with them over their religious problems. When he became priest he sang the Mass. And for a decade and a half he was a member of the choir, chanting the Psalms for hours every day with dedication and insight.

It seems to me that this combination of conversational silence and liturgical sound had a profound effect on Merton as a writer, encouraging him to continue his literary activity because it filled the gap of silence in his personal life: he conversed with people out in the world instead of with his immediate companions. But it also helped to shape the very character of his work, both poetry and prose. In fact it gives much of that work a curious flavour of archaic devotionalism, since in his writings up to the middle 1950s Merton was often using the imagery and the language associated with a way of religious life that had once belonged to many but which when he entered Gethsemani was already the province of only a small minority even among Catholics, a minority that has decreased even more dramatically with the turn of the Church since Vatican II in the direction of a more activist ministry. I am not talking merely of the hagiographies which adopted the pietistic tone customary in traditional lives of the saints, or of books

like *The Waters of Siloe,* a history of the Cistercian Order written
at the request of Merton's superiors and obediently couched in
acceptable form. I am talking rather of the characteristics that
attracted many of its readers to *The Seven Storey Mountain,* his
first prose work that was not written specifically with an eye to the
needs of the Order. They saw it with the same romantic view that
readers of previous generations had applied to historical novels
of the middle ages; to them it was important not as the account
of a contemporary life, or for its rather thin theology, or even as
the account of a religious experience they might live through
vicariously or even imitate, but most of all as an episode reminis-
cent of an idealized mediaeval past, a kind of retelling of the story
of St. Francis in the form — to quote the description on my paperback copy — of "the biography of a young man who lived an exciting, worldly life until the age of twenty-six, when he entered a
Trappist monastery."

Yet Merton himself was not in the same sense a romantic. He
lived the mediaeval monastic life of the Trappists, which now in
1978 is already a thing of the past, to the full and as if he were
living it in the eternal present, and though in later years he recognized that he had outgrown the need for its cenobitic aspects,
which was why he finally retired to his hermitage and then took
the even more unusual step for an enclosed monk of embarking
on his great Asian journey, he never denied the value of the discipline he had endured and so passionately accepted. "It is precisely
in familiarity with liturgical worship and moral discipline," he said
in 1966, "that the beginner finds his identity, gains a certain con-
fidence from his spiritual practice and learns to believe that the
spiritual life has a goal that is definitely possible of attainment."
And on several occasions, at intervals throughout his monastic
life, he defended obedience to the harsh mediaeval rules on the
grounds that the paradoxical result was spiritual freedom, since
obedience to the rules and participation in the liturgy lessened
the distractions created by the demands of the personal self and
thus liberated the true self.

Nor does this sacramental mediaevalism detract from the
quality of the best of Merton's work during his early monastic
period; in fact it does not really affect a good proportion of that

work, including the more restrained works of the contemplative experience and the spare poetry of the eremitic life which I shall call "the poetry of the desert" as distinct from the much more ornate work which I shall call "the poetry of the choir."

It is the poetry of the choir, which belongs peculiarly to the cenobitic side of Merton's monastic life, that I shall now discuss — and particularly in relation to his role as a choir monk and to his celebration of the Mass as a priest, for as aspects of Merton in his monastic setting the chorister, the priest and the poet come very close together.

A little over a decade after he entered Gethsemani, Merton wrote a little book on the Psalms. He had reason to know the subject well, since every week the choir of Gethsemani would chant its majestic Gregorian way through all the hundred and fifty Psalms, and in *Bread in the Wilderness* he celebrated their poetic beauty, their wisdom, their typological anticipations of the events of Christ's life on earth and the creation of the Church, and their utility, together with the Mass, in the contemplative's quest. "If a contemplative," he warns, "were to regard the Mass and Office as secondary in his interior life, he would run a serious risk of coming to a standstill in his prayer, and even of falling into illusion." He saw the Psalms in terms of eschatology — the foretelling of the last days, the Parousia: "All Scriptural types point to the last end, the crowning of Christ's work, the establishment of His Kingdom." And he saw them — as prayer and praise — in terms of an ecstasy that is both communal and individual, an ecstasy that in one amazing passage of *Bread in the Wilderness* Merton describes in intensely personal terms:

> We too, when we chant these verses as the old saints must have chanted them, experience the truth which the Fathers reveal to us in their writings. We find out that when we bring our own sorrows and desires and hopes and fears to God and plunge them all into the sorrows and hopes of the mysterious One who sings this Psalm, a kind of transubstantiation is effected. We have put all that we have — or rather all our poverty, all that we have not — into the hands of Christ. He who is Everything and has everything pronounces over our gift words of His own. Consecrated by contact with the poverty He assumed to deliver us, we find that in His

poverty our poverty becomes infinite riches; in His sufferings our defeats are transubstantiated into victory, and His death becomes our everlasting life.

What has happened? We have been transformed. The process is more than a tragic *catharsis*. This is more than the psychological impact of a work of art, in which our emotions, clenched in a dramatic crisis, have been sprung, have been released, and have achieved a vital fulfilment by a successful poetic solution of the problem in which we have allowed ourselves to become emotionally involved. There is something much deeper. It is a spiritual solution. It is a kind of death and a sea-change, operated as it were at the bottom of a spiritual ocean, because it can just as well happen to us when the Psalm, having become insipid to us by continual repetition, has ceased to have any immediate artistic appeal. And I may add that it might even happen to someone who has never quite been attuned to the full poetic quality of the Psalms.

This transformation is operated in us by the power of the Holy Spirit Who lives and acts in the word He has inspired. He, if you like, is the poet. But He also is the poetry. Or rather Christ, Whose Spirit He is, is the poetry of the Psalms. But the Holy Spirit, besides being the artist, is also the spectator. He is at the same time the poet, the poetry and the reader of the poetry; the music and the musician, the singer and the hearer. The peculiar mystical impact with which certain verses of Psalms suddenly produce this silent depth-charge in the heart of the contemplative is only to be accounted for by the fact that we, in the Spirit, recognize the Spirit singing in ourselves.

This is clearly an occasion for the suspending of disbelief. It is difficult for the nonbeliever, except aesthetically, to empathize with such an experience, and it is equally difficult to imagine such an experience being achieved while chanting the psalms on a Sunday morning in a comfortable Protestant church. But envisage the setting at Gethsemani: a company of haggard men who have not slept well or eaten fully since the last midday, and the sheer volume of rhythmic sound echoing in the vaulted space: the experience, as Merton put it later in the same book, of "hearing twenty or fifty or a hundred voices all blending into one voice, crying out to God in the first person singular," and crying out in the dark silent hours of the night. The psychological and physical preconditions of ecstasy are understood in many religions, primitive and sophisticated; we have to take in trust anew in every case the visionary results of such occasions when the mind is broken open to light.

Merton speaks in this passage of the poetic quality of the Psalms, and at another point in *Bread in the Wilderness* he declares that "The Psalms are the new song, the canticum novum, the song of those who have been reborn in the new creation." I believe that Merton considered the works which I describe as the poems of the choir — and which I shall shortly discuss — to be the songs of his own rebirth into the contemplative life, and for this reason it is important to consider the statement on poetry and religion which he includes in the chapter entitled "Poetry, Symbolism and Typology."

He begins with a virtually aestheticist statement on the autonomy of poetry, a statement that appears less surprising when one remembers that he accorded the artist a special access to truth analogous to that of the contemplative:

> . . . In poetry, words are charged with meaning in a far different way than are the words in a piece of scientific prose. The words of a poem are not merely the signs of concepts: they are also rich in affective and spiritual associations. The poet uses words not merely to make declarations, statements of fact. That is usually the last thing that concerns him. He seeks above all to put words together in such a way that they exercise a mysterious and vital reactivity among themselves, and so release their secret content of associations to produce in the reader an experience that enriches the depths of his spirit in a manner quite unique. A good poem induces an experience that could not be produced by any other combination of words. It is therefore an entity that stands by itself, graced with an individuality that marks it off from every other work of art. Like all great works of art, true poems seem to live by a life entirely their own. What we must seek in a poem is therefore not an accidental reference to something outside itself: we must seek this inner principle of individuality and of life which is its soul, or "form." What the poem actually "means" can only be summed up in the whole content of poetic experience which it is capable of producing in the reader. This total poetic experience is what the poet is trying to communicate to the rest of the world.

From this statement, to which no symbolist from Verlaine to
Yeats would be likely to take exception, it is clear that Merton's
attitude towards the art which his destiny forced him to practise
had not changed materially since the pre-monastic days when he
remarked, in *The Secular Journal,* that: "We should stop demanding what the Communists demand of plays and books: that
they conform to some abstract set of principles imposed upon
them from the outside, not that they should merely tell the truth
in their own terms and be good books or plays." Whatever gentle
pressure may have been put on Merton to write prose works that
would specifically serve the interests of the Cistercian Order, there
is nothing to suggest that his spiritual directors interfered with his
poetry except to the extent of encouraging him to continue writing
it. There is no doubt, if we compare his verse with the prose
journals he kept at the same time as he wrote the poems of the
choir, that the poems gave forth the real enthusiasms and ecstasies of his earlier years as a monk, those years when he pushed his
studies and his spiritual exercises so far that he suffered two serious
physical and nervous collapses—one at the end of his novitiate
and the other after his ordination as a priest—whose effects lasted
for months. All this gives special importance to later passages in
Bread in the Wilderness where Merton discusses the criteria for
poetry that will be both religious and authentic. He distinguishes
religious poetry from devotional poetry. The first springs from "a
true religious experience," by which Merton is careful to say that
he does not "necessarily mean a mystical experience." "Devotional
poetry is verse which manipulates religious themes and which
does so, perhaps, even on a truly poetic level. But the experiential
content of the poem is at best poetic only. Sometimes it is not
even that." Such poetry may be piously inspired, it may be produced for a true religious purpose, it may be directed towards the
salvation of souls (though, as Merton remarks, it is likely to irri-
tate the souls "who really need salvation"). He continues:

> A truly religious poem is not born merely of a religious pur-
> pose. Neither poetry nor contemplation is built out of good in-
> tentions. Indeed, a poem that springs from no deeper spiritual need
> than a devout intention will necessarily appear to be at the same

time forced and tame. Art that is simply "willed" is not art, and it tends to have the same disquieting effect upon the reader as forced piety and religious strain in those who are trying hard to be contemplatives, as if infused contemplation were the result of human effort rather than a gift of God. . . . The Psalms, on the other hand, are at the same time the simplest and the greatest of all religious poems.

He sees the virtues of the Psalms not merely in the authenticity of their experiential content, the grandeur of their ecstasies, but also in the symbolism that gives them form, and this symbolism takes two aspects: there is the typological symbolism, the symbols in which believers can see the presaging of Christian history, and the cosmic symbolism that concerns the revelation of God to man through nature and which is not the exclusive property of Christianity or any other single religion. To learn *"how to see and respect the visible creation* which mirrors the glory and the perfections of the invisible God"* is — Merton remarks in *The Monastic Journey* — a necessary beginning on the contemplative's path, but — as he implies in *Bread in the Wilderness* — it is also a necessary part of the poet's function.

> Light and darkness, sun and moon, stars and planets, trees, beasts, whales, fishes and birds of the air, all these things in the world around us and the whole natural economy in which they have their place have impressed themselves upon the spirit of man in such a way that they naturally tend to mean to him much more than they mean in themselves. That is why, for example, they enter so mysteriously into the substance of our poetry, of our visions and of our dreams.

And it is because our modern civilization has submerged the kind of life in which such symbols have significance that so many modern poets find their symbols in "the moonlit cemeteries of surrealism," symbols of "starvation, madness, frustration and death."

There are many poems of the choir in which one can see in practice the concepts of true religious poetry that Merton adumbrated in *Bread in the Wilderness*. They occur mainly in the first four volumes he published: *Thirty Poems* (1944), *A Man in the*

Divided Sea (1946), *Figures for an Apocalypse* (1947) and *The Tears of the Blind Lions* (1949). Few poems of this kind were written by Merton in the 1950s, and none occur in the sharply different books of verse that began to appear with the "anti-poem," *Original Child Bomb*, in 1962. By this time, as we shall see, Merton himself had taken up poetic residence very near "the moonlit cemeteries of surrealism."

Rather than attempting a general survey of all the poems of the choir, I have chosen a few examples from Merton's more ceno-bitic poems. Almost ideally typical is "A Whitsun Canticle" (*A Man in the Divided Sea*), in which the influence of psalmody is very strong indeed. It is a poem of laudation in which the poet calls upon man and nature to praise God, and in which he addresses the Father and the Holy Spirit. At the beginning the ascension of Christ is evoked, then the descent of the pentecostal fires and the rejoicing of the disciples:

> Father, Father, Whom we thought so hidden
> Somewhere behind the jealous walls of Mars,
> Oh how You visit us, at the deep roots of life,
> With glad reprisals.

Men's minds and the world itself are exhorted to sing in rejoicing as the cosmos rejoices in all its aspects, and finally, in the last three stanzas, the Holy Spirit is invoked. This last portion of the poem, somewhat less than half, I quote in full to give a sense of the quality of the whole canticle.

> O Holy Spirit, hear, we call Your Name aloud,
> We speak You plain and humble in the terms of prayer,
> Whatever talk You grant us:
> One day we run among the rocks as lithe as lions,
> But it is better that, the next, You tame our jubilee,
> And prune our praises lean as supplication:
> Make us believe You better in the crazy desert,
> And seek You better in the skipping heat,
> Follow Your messages until we beat our heads
> Against the jazz of the horizon.
> We'll find You there as much as in the caves of shade,
> The grass and springs of the oasis:

But only wring us always, at the center of our inward earth,
Artesian secrets for the roots of love.

But if we walk up to the waist
In the green exultation of the growing harvest,
And if, in the ripe days, the sheaves and increase,
Springing to life on the off-beat of the tractor's congas
Bound from the bouncing binder light as lambs:
Or if we fly, like doves, to the blue woods and consolations
Of the peaceful August,
And in high hiding ring our muffled bells:
Forgive us, always, if our clumsy wills,
Reeling with the possession of so pure a pleasure,
Stumble and break the bottles of our Pentecost.

ENVOI
Beloved Spirit, you are all the prudence and the power
That change our dust and nothing into fields and fruits:
Enfold our lives forever in the compass of Your peaceful hills.
Build us a monastery, yes, forever,
(Stones of our cloister lofty as transparent air
And wonderful as light)
In the full fields of gentle Heaven.
Build us our cells forever in Your Mercy's woods:
Then tell Orion and Andromeda our hearts are heavens
And that our eyes are light-years deep,
Sounding Your will, Your peace, in its unbounded fathoms:
Oh balance all our turning orbits, till that morning,
Upon the center and the level of Your holy love:
Then lock our souls forever in the nucleus of its Law.

One is immediately impressed by the sustained tone of joy,
breathless, beyond breath, that provides the dominant feeling to
the poem. It is a song of praise, an invocation of the Paraclete,
an evocation of the special pentecostal ecstasy. But in more than
spirit is the Canticle in the true psalmodic tradition; the imagery,
the diction, the prosody being there also. Here and there modern
images occur—"jazz of the horizon," "artesian secrets," "the tractor's congas"—and strangely enough they do not seem to clash
with the rest of the poem, which means that it is archaic rather
than archaicist, emerging from a special reclusive world that has

admitted only a few features of modernity into itself but has accepted them unselfconsciously. In general the imagery tends to vary in new ways the traditional and biblical: "His garments fluttered like a thousand flags," "their arrows of tremendous news," "we run among the rocks as lithe as lions." It is, in accordance with Merton's poetic principles, concrete and strongly visual imagery whose natural authenticity is meant, like that of the psalmist, to form a window through which the inner spiritual reality of the poem may shine.

Formally, the influence of the Psalms can be seen in many features of the Canticle: in the invocatory manner ("O Holy Spirit, hear, we call Your Name aloud"); in the frequency of grammatical repetitions ("Minds, minds, sing like spring / To see the hills... / World, world, sing like spring / To hear the harvests..."); and especially in the predilection, common to all the poems of the choir, for the kind of long, sustained and rather leaping lines that Merton was accustomed to chanting to the magnificent Gregorian chants:

> Behold the birds, released like angels, from those leafy palaces
> With fire and blue and red-gold splashing in their painted wings...
>
> But only wring us always, at the center of our inward earth...
>
> Sounding Your will, Your peace, in its unbounded fathoms...

Finally, the Canticle displays a characteristic common to many of the poems of the choir which I can only describe — without pejorative intent — as loudness. It is the sound — sometimes unnerving to the mere listener — of men chanting in thundering tones their release from ordinary silence into the silence beyond sound, and perhaps more than anything else it distinguishes poems of this kind from those poems of the inner silence which I call Merton's poems of the desert.

It may be that in my desire to find a typical example of the poems of the choir I have picked one that carries the evocation of gladness to the point of stridency. There are others in which the more static grandeurs of the monastic tradition, which the great mediaeval conventual churches expressed, are re-evoked, and meditative or lyrically evocative passages counterpoint the songs of joy. An excellent example — and in my view one of the best of Merton's poems of the choir — is "Rievaulx: St. Ailred," from *Figures for an Apocalypse*.

Rievaulx was the great Cistercian abbey in the Yorkshire dales whose church still stands in ruins as one of the purest examples of English Gothic architecture. I have come across no hint that Merton visited Rievaulx when he was young in England, but he certainly went to the Cistercian abbey at Beaulieu in Hampshire, and in *The Seven Storey Mountain* he recorded that he walked through the ruins and — "in the usual picnic spirit" — "tasted a little of the silence and peacefulness of the greensward under the trees" but that as yet he cared little about "monks and monasteries." Perhaps, nevertheless, a visual memory remained of this and other English ruins, and bore fruit in the lines where Merton first evokes the landscape of the dales that were Rievaulx's setting.

> Once when the white clouds praised you, Yorkshire,
> Flying before the sun, flying before the eastern wind,
> What greenness grew along the waters,
> Flowering in the valleys of the purple moor . . .
>
> The viewless wind came walking on the land like a Messiah
> Spending the thin scent of the russet heather,
> Lauding the flowering gorse and the green broom:
> Because this was your spring.
> The sky had new-discovered you, and looked and loved you
> Began to teach you songs to sing upon the day of your espousal.
> So Rievaulx raised her white cathedral in the wilderness
> Arising in her strength and newness beautiful as Judith.

As the poem continues Merton mingles the tale of the abbey's building with references to the birds and the spring sprouting of the woodlands, until the abbey stands complete and the poem as choir bursts forth in the chant of accomplishment.

> The sun that plays in the amazing church
> Melts all the rigor of those cowls as grey as stone —
> Or in the evening gloom that clouds them through those tintless
>   panes,
> The choirs fall down in tidal waves

And thunder on the darkened forms in a white surf of *Glorias:*
And thence we see the tribes, the tribes go up
To their Jerusalem
Out of the quiet tumult of their fierce Gregorian death!

There is much in a poem like this of the joy in God's creation which in the English tradition has ever since the late middle ages brought nature poetry and religious poetry so close together and even in recent decades has made many poets, such an Andrew Young, Norman Nicholson and Edwin Muir (on whom Merton wrote with great sympathy), practitioners of both. An even more impressive example of this kind of combination—a poem that hovers on the verge between the poetry of the desert and the poetry of the choir (but by its fullness of tone must be regarded as belonging to the latter category)—is "Natural History," also from *Figures for an Apocalypse,* in which, somewhat in the manner of the seventeenth-century metaphysicals, Merton meditates on the grubs he sees, on a monastery wall in autumn, undergoing their metamorphosis into pupae. He evokes the grey wall, overhung with honeysuckle, and the "creeping things which . . . in the wise diligence of an ascetic season, / Have worked their small momentous wonder, / Prepared their winter's sleep."

There is a lesson here, he suggests, as he asks who directed "these six or seven creepers" to find this haven and, as grubs at least, to die.

Leaving all leaves and grasses and the smaller flowers
And all their haunts unseen and summer pastures
They do not stay to study Your command, Your mystery,
That this, the only thing they know, must cease
And they must seal themselves in silences and sleep.
See with what zeal they wrestle off their ancient, tawny life
And fight with all their might to end their private histories
And lock their days in the cocoon.

Merton concludes that "all creation teaches us some way of prayer," and in the metamorphosis of the grubs he sees, as it were, the type of man's transformation, of his spiritual death with the promise of rebirth.

Here on the Trappist wall, beside the cemetery,
Two figures, death and contemplation,
Write themselves out before us in the easy sun
Where everything that moves is full of mystical theology.

Shall we still fear the fight that wrests our way
Free from the vesture of our ancient days,
Killing the prisoner, Adam, in us,
And laying us away to sleep a space, in the transforming Christ?

While one cannot class this as a poem out of its time, it is nevertheless the kind of poem that is less likely to be written in the twentieth century, except in a situation like a monastery, than in the seventeenth century. And there is no doubt that Merton learned a great deal from the religious poets of that time — from Vaughan and Traherne, from Donne and Crashaw — as he also did from Blake, but perhaps, as we shall later see, the lessons of the metaphysicals emerge more clearly in his poetry of the desert. It is the ecstatic expansiveness of the Psalms that mainly rules the poems of the choir, and in these works prevents Merton from applying that lesson of intensity conveyed through density and conciseness which poets like Donne can teach.

There is one striking point where Merton and Donne seem to come together — and do indeed in the matter of their content — yet are far apart in the degree of ultimate achievement. The Merton poem is his "Hymn for the Feast of Duns Scotus," (*The Tears of the Blind Lions*) in which he discusses Scotus on the Trinity, and says how the Scholastic's book "burns me like a branding iron!" He continues:

For the sound of my Beloved,
The voice of the sound of my Three Beloved
(One of my Three of my One Beloved)
Comes down out of the heavenly depths
And hits my heart like thunder:
And lo! I am alive and dead
With heart held fast in that Three-Personed Love.

And lo! God, my God!
Look! Look! I travel in Thy Strength
I swing in the grasp of Thy Love, Thy great Love's One Strength,
I run Thy swift ways, Thy straightest rails
Until my life becomes Thy Life and sails or rides like an express!

This is good in its own way as a piece of rhapsodic verse, of psalmody modernized by a touch of Spenderian railway imagery, but how far it is from greatness we realize when we think of Donne and our mind quails at the agony of "Batter my heart, three-person'd God; for, you / As yet but knock, breathe, shine, and seek to mend . . ."

The poems of the choir, of course, were not the only kinds of poem that Merton was writing during those years when his most dominant concern was the cenobitic life. Other facets of his mind were already making their demands and creating their special kinds of poetry — the poetry of the desert to express the eremitic urge, poems about the iniquity of the metropolis and its culture (like "Figures for an Apocalypse") to sustain his socially critical vision, and here and there a poem out of classical antiquity that kept alive his sense of the truth in other traditions. These I shall come to in their proper places.

Meanwhile there remains one aspect of Merton's life as a monk in the cenobium that was certainly as important in his mind and heart as his participation in the choir. That was his priesthood. Monks are not necessarily priests. In the early mediaeval abbeys, in fact, the vast majority were simple brothers with a small number of ordained priests to look after their spiritual needs and conduct the liturgy. In more recent centuries the monastic liturgy has grown in complexity and a much larger number of novices have become scholastics after their preparatory period and have gone on to ordination. A priest in a monastery takes his equal share of the general work, and spends his hours in the choir like any other monk, but his special role is notably different from that of a secular priest who has pastoral duties to the flock in his charge; the monastic priest's activities are concentrated mainly on sustaining the frequent celebration of the Mass.

In *The Seven Storey Mountain* Merton tells how, when he first visited Gethsemani as a retreatant, he followed the silent walkers into the "great dark church, where, in little chapels, all round the ambulatory behind the great altar, chapels that were caves of dim candlelight, Mass was simultaneously beginning at many altars."

He grasped immediately the importance of the Mass in the monastic pattern. He saw it ever after, as he says in *Bread in the Wilderness,* as "the central mystery of the whole Christian economy, since it is the Sacrifice in which Christ offers Himself to the Father for the Sins of the World." He saw the Mass as producing "a unity of the faithful in charity" which "is the full expression of the Mystery of Christ on Earth," and for all his eremitic inclinations, he warned the contemplative, as we have seen, against regarding the Mass, or any other part of the liturgy, "as secondary to his interior life." Never, to the end and whatever his opinions on reformation within the monastic order, did Merton give up his view of the centrality of the Mass as the realization of Christ's sacrifice. In the last years, the years of his longed-for reclusion, he still celebrated Mass at the altar with its Orthodox icons which he had arranged in his hermitage, and during his last journey he took every opportunity that offered itself to conduct the rite in the remote little Catholic churches of Asia, in Madras, in Darjeeling, wherever he found them.

Merton knew from the beginning that for him the vocation of monk could only be complete if he became a priest. Indeed, his desire to be a priest pre-dated his decision to enter a contemplative order. "My priestly ordination was, I felt, the one great secret for which I had been born," he says in *The Sign of Jonas.* "Ten years before I was ordained, when I was in the world, and seemed to be one of the men in the world most unlikely to become a priest, I had suddenly realized that for me ordination to the priesthood was, in fact, a matter of life or death, heaven or hell. As I finally came within sight of this perfect meeting with the inscrutable will of God, my vocation became clear. It was a mercy and a secret which were so purely mine that at first I intended to speak of them to no one."

Merton took his solemn monastic vows in 1947, and then proceeded up the ladder of the orders — became exorcist and acolyte, sub-deacon and deacon, playing at each stage his different and growing role in the drama of the Mass—until in 1949 he was finally ordained as a priest. It was a time of doubts and ecstatic certainties, of agonies and joys, so intense that at the end, when it was all complete, Merton collapsed into a long illness, yet with a sense of having been changed utterly by this sealing of his vocation.

> So the grace of my priesthood, the greatest of my life, was to me something far greater than a momentary flight above the monotonous lowlands of an everyday existence. It permanently transformed my ordinary, everyday life. It was a transfiguration of all simple and usual things, an elevation of the plainest and most natural acts to the level of the sublime. It showed me that the charity of God was sufficient to transform earth into heaven. For God is Charity, and Charity is Heaven. (*The Sign of Jonas*)

Strangely enough, there is little in Merton's poetry that celebrates his priesthood. Perhaps the experience of the Mass was poetry enough, a vocation that could not be rendered in terms of another vocation. It is in *The Sign of Jonas,* the spiritual journal that Merton kept from 1946 to 1953, that we find—mingled with the narrative of monastic life—the accounts of his state of mind at this vital time of completing his novitiate and moving forward into priesthood and into a central role in the running of the abbey as Master of Scholastics.

Apart from his poems of the choir, and the books I have mentioned earlier in this chapter, *The Seven Storey Mountain* and *The Sign of Jonas* are the most important—as they are without exception the most informative—of the works produced by Merton as a cenobitic monk, as the loyal and obediently functioning (despite his hankering after the hermitage) member of a rigorous monastic community.

Though in content *The Seven Storey Mountain* deals for the most part with Merton's pre-monastic life, it is best considered in the monastic context, since it was written entirely at Gethsemani, and not completed until 1947, after Merton had been in the monastery for almost six years. It is therefore a life seen from within the cenobitic enclosure, and the kind of hindsight that it projects is inevitably coloured by the fact that as he wrote the book Merton was striving with a convert's zeal to become the perfect monk. It is clearly modelled on St. Augustine's *Confessions,* which Merton had read even before his conversion, and everything is seen in the light of the end of the story, so that—unlike Merton's journals—it is not a progressive account of development. Every autobiography, of course, is shaped inevitably by the time in which the author writes it and his state of mind at that time. But there is something more sharply intentional about the shaping of a confessional autobiography.

We do not have to look very closely at *The Seven Storey Mountain* to see how latter-day judgements shape the accounts of incident after incident, from the rather cold portrayal of Merton's austere Quaker mother, through the enthusiastic treatment of France—with its mediaeval relics and its Christian tradition—as a kind of unrecognized preparation for conversion and the monastic life, and the obviously tinted account of the 1933 visit to Rome, down to the denigration of apostate England, the denunciation of its flaccid Anglicanism and the positively grotesque representation of Cambridge as an evil place when all Merton really has to tell us is of his own youthful follies and weaknesses:

> Perhaps to you the atmosphere of Cambridge is neither dark nor sinister. Perhaps you were never there except in May. You never saw anything but the thin Spring sun half veiled in the mists and blossoms of the gardens along the Backs, smiling on the lavender bricks and stones of Trinity and St. John's, or my own college, Clare.
>
> I am even willing to admit that some people might live there for three years, or even a lifetime, so protected that they never sense the sweet stench of corruption that is all around them—the keen, thin scent of decay that pervades everything and accuses with a terrible accusation the superficial youthfulness, the abounding undergraduate noise that fills those ancient buildings. But for me, with my blind appetites, it was impossible that I should not rush in and take a huge bite of this rotten fruit. The bitter taste is still with me after not a few years.

There are many passages of this kind and worse that stud and mar the book: mini-sermons masking as reflections, bigoted dismissals of any Christian way other than the Catholic, and denunciations of "filthy" novels that turn out to be the works of writers like Gide and Hemingway. This kind of writing, which appealed to a large number of pietistic Catholics in the 1940s and 1950s, is as silly as it is distasteful, and it is among the worst of Merton's prose. Yet such passages stand in peculiar isolation within the general text, and one can only assume that in writing them Merton was affected by the hagiographic manner he was induced to adopt in writing his lives of the saints, a manner in which he became for the time being a religious equivalent of a Communist convert doing hack work for the party. Certainly Merton himself was by no means unembarrassed by much in *The Seven Storey Mountain*. In the 1960s he saw the Merton who had written the book as a "superficially pious, rather rigid and somewhat narrow-minded young monk" — a person already "dead" to him — and his judgement was as fair as anyone could ask.

Yet there are good things in *The Seven Storey Mountain*. Merton has a serviceable and often vivid narrative manner, and the personages of his life, seen with the detachment of the writer's essential loneliness, are sharply portrayed. The book has its own bittersweet humour, and, perhaps most important of all, it is one of the most telling of the many accounts we have had of the hard pilgrimages of the young men and women of the Thirties. Many of them — Greene, Auden, Kathleen Raine, Muggeridge — arrived in the same general terrain as Merton, though few took so extreme a step away from the familiar world as to enter a monastery. The agonies of conversion to any faith are always fascinating, perhaps because we never know when we ourselves may be inexplicably called to endure them, and in Merton's case the genuine passion usually outweighs the callow opinionatedness.

The title *The Seven Storey Mountain* of course refers to purgatory as Dante described it, though some recent readers familiar with Merton's oriental interests have found a certain appropriateness in the fact that holy places in Asia, like the great Buddhist complex of Borobodur in Java, are often planned in seven layers as representations of the mythical Mount Meru, the seven-storeyed symbol of the cosmos. Merton was likening his earthly travails to Purgatory, but when he later wrote *The Sign of Jonas* he was more wryly and humorously modest, using the fate of Jonas — or Jonah — whom the whale carried where God — not he—wanted him to be, as an ironic symbol of his own monastic life which, though he willed otherwise, had kept him from the reclusion he wished to gain and had forced him to continue the writing he wished to abandon.

The Sign of Jonas is a journal of episodes and reflections, and, as always, the mosaic form suits Merton's peculiar talent. A subject need never be exhausted, since the form always gives time and space for an afterthought, but by the same token a subject need not be circumscribed within a closed mental pattern. These were crucial years for Merton, when he entered into the fullness of monastic life, but they were also years when his mind began to expand, to lose its restrictiveness, to reach out laterally towards other minds and traditions.

Once again, in *The Sign of Jonas,* there are really two styles and manners of perception at work. On the one hand, there is the Merton who is interested in every aspect of the physical world — the lover of God's creation in a very similar way to Hopkins — who writes vividly on the routines of the monastery, on the kinds of work he does, on his fellow monks, on the monastery as an actual place, and on the farm and forest to which he devotes a great deal of lyrical description that reminds us he was always an admirer of Henry David Thoreau. In all this one has the impression of an unclouded and genial mind at work, a mind whose essential charity emerges in an unwillingness to judge, for one feature absent from *The Sign of Jonas* is any reference to the kind of personal acrimonies which — as anyone who has lived in a community of any kind will know — must occur in monasteries as they do in similar secular settings.

But interspersed with this narrative of the visible world are the accounts of Merton's state of mind regarding his vocation. Sometimes he discourses very rationally on the problems of the contemplative within a cenobitic community, and rather less often he engages in serious theological speculation. But there are also the occasions when he tries to record ecstatic moments in his spiritual progress, and here it is evident that prose is rarely adequate to the task. One passage is especially moving because in the middle of it Merton breaks down to complain of the inadequacy of words to express what he intends:

Day after day I am more and more aware that I am anything but my everyday self at the altar: this consciousness of innocence is really a sense of replacement. I am superseded by One in Whom I am fully real. Another has taken over my identity (or He has revealed it), and this Other is a tremendous infancy. And I stand at the altar—excuse the language, these words should not be extraordinary—I stand at the altar with my eyes all washed in the light that is eternity, and I become one who is agelessly reborn. I am sorry for this language. There are no words I know of simple enough to describe such a thing, except that every day I am a day old, and at the altar I am the Child Who is God and yet when it is all over I have to say *Lux in tenebris lucet et tenebrae eam non comprehenderunt* and I have to fall back into my own, in *my* poor *"propria"* which cannot receive Him altogether.

Diaries and journals tend to be like mirrors in their effect on their writers. There is an almost irresistible temptation to put on our best faces, or sometimes to make an ugly face for effect, and to tidy up our expressions as well as our hair. Such seems often the case in *The Sign of Jonas;* there is a formal neatness, a worked-on polish about many passages which reminds us that to Merton his journals were not just diaries for the spontaneous notation of events and thoughts on the wing but rather books in the making to which he entrusted considered thought, in which he worked out that thought, and in which he would sometimes record experiences in a way which shows the artist very carefully at work. This neatness appears in the long meditative passages that often build up into elaborate poetic artifacts. One occurs on Shrove Tuesday, 1952. Merton is sitting outside the walls of the monastery enclosure at Gethsemani:

> The blue elm tree near at hand and the light blue hills in the distance: the red bare clay where I am supposed to plant some shade trees: these are before me as I sit in the sun for a free half hour between direction and work. Tomorrow is Ash Wednesday and today, as I sit in the sun, big blue and purple fish swim past me in the darkness of my empty mind. This sea which opens within me as soon as I close my eyes. Delightful darkness, delightful sun, shining on a world which, for all I care, has already ended.

He goes on to meditate on the "different levels of depth"

where the fish swim, which are different levels of awareness. There is the "troubled surface of the sea," the world of action. There is the darkness, the "cave of the inner being" where there is peace and where strange creatures swim. There is the third level of spiritual awareness where positive life swims in a "rich darkness which is no longer thick like water, but pure like air." And this is "the holy cellar of my mortal existence, which opens into the sky. . . . It is a strange awakening to find the sky inside you and beneath you and above you and all around you so that your spirit is one with the sky, and all is positive night."

The Sign of Jonas ends with an even more elaborate meditation entitled "Fire Watch, July 4, 1952," in which Merton takes his turn as monastic night watchman, and, as he wanders around the buildings of the abbey with his heavy clock, projects himself into a dual state of recollection (memory and concentration alike) and relates each place to the history of the community and to his own inner history, which have become intertwined beyond disentanglement. It is a splendidly evocative essay in spiritual autobiography.

The presence of such consciously crafted passages in *The Sign of Jonas* is itself a sign that Merton by now has finally reconciled his two vocations, and has recognized the kinship of the aesthetic and the spiritual and how they serve each other. Indeed, in *No Man Is an Island,* a book on the religious life which he wrote shortly afterwards, he faces the issue directly, talking of the liberating nature of the aesthetic experience: "Art enables us to find ourselves and lose ourselves at the same time. The mind that responds to the intellectual and spiritual values that lie hidden in a poem, a painting, or a piece of music, discovers a spiritual vitality that lifts it above itself, takes it out of itself, and makes it present to itself on a level of being that it did not know it could ever achieve."

But art, Merton continues, "is not an end in itself." It is in its own manner a way to God. "The genius of the artist finds its way by the affinity of creative sympathy, or connaturality, into the living law that rules the universe. This law is nothing but the secret gravitation that draws all things to God as to their center. Since all true art lays bare the action of this same law in the depths of our own nature, it makes us alive to the tremendous mystery of being, in which we ourselves, together with all other living and existing things, come forth from the depths of God and return again to Him."

For Merton the role of the monk and the role of the poet had come together, each serving the other and both, in his belief, serving God. And whatever the temptations of literary fame, he remained faithful to the monastery to the end of his days. In many ways he changed and relaxed his views. He ceased to despise other Christian ways. He recognized that the active ministry, which he had once thought inferior to the contemplative way, was in its own manner a form of contemplation and no less acceptable than the way of the monk. He favoured changes in monastic customs if not in the basic rule, and he encouraged other kinds of reclusion in a secular setting as perhaps offering something that the regular cenobitic life did not, for as he remarked in *The Monastic Journey*, "the Holy Spirit speaks in many ways and one of the ways in which He speaks is precisely through the *needs*, the *poverty*, the *limitation* of our fellow men."

But he still believed that the monastic community and he as a monk had a special and indispensible role of mediation with the divine and of exploring that wilderness of the heart where the powers of evil and good are most strongly present, the desert within and without: "the singing desert," as he called it in his poems; "the holy desert."

4

The Desert

The wasteland is one of the inescapable concepts in modern literature. T. S. Eliot first articulated it in the poem of that title which he published more than fifty years ago. *The Waste Land* has remained one of the most potent evocations of the alienation which is the great sickness of our world, but others had diagnosed the condition before Eliot, and what Marx and Nietzsche saw in our way of life, without being able to perceive a right solution, is not very much different from the insights of Christian existentialists from Kierkegaard down to Merton.

Merton called himself an existentialist. In his rejection of idealism; in his insistence on the individual and the particular (each man having to face his own death, having to make his own encounter with God); in his intuitive distrust of abstract metaphysics in favour of an experiential investigation of being; in his rejection of all extreme doctrines of necessity and predestination; in his insistence on freedom of will and hence on the responsibility of choice; and in his equal understanding of the limitations of choice that living in the world imposed, he has a good claim to the title. Like Kierkegaard he knew the "fear and trembling" of the spiritual life. In later years especially he tended to see the human predicament in the very terms used by the existentialists, and there are more than echoes of Kierkegaard's concept of "dread" and Sartre's of "nausea" in a late work like *Contemplative Prayer*, which was written in Merton's last year and published after his death. Indeed, when he talks of the way prayer can expose to us the truth about ourselves, he uses the very words of Sartre and Kierkegaard and presents a mental situation remarkably like that which results from the meditations of existentialists on the human condition:

> ...the dimensions of prayer in solitude are those of man's ordinary anguish, his self-searching, his moments of nausea at his own vanity, falsity and capacity for betrayal. Far from establishing one in unassailable narcissistic security, the way of prayer brings us face to face with the sham and indignity of the false self that seeks to live for itself alone and to enjoy the "consolation of prayer" for its own sake....
>
> ... This self-questioning can never be without a certain existential "dread" — a sense of insecurity, of "lostness," of exile, of sin. A sense that one has somehow been untrue not so much to abstract moral or social norms but to one's own inmost truth. "Dread" in this sense is not simply a childish fear of retribution, or a naive guilt, a fear of violating taboos. It is the profound awareness that one is capable of ultimate bad faith with himself and with others; that one is living a lie.

Later in the same book, Merton emphasizes his closeness to a great modern thinker and writer who was very near to the existentialists although he refused to be identified with them, Albert Camus: "The monk confronts his own humanity and that of his world at the deepest and most central point where the void seems to open out into black despair. The monk confronts this serious possibility, and rejects it, as Camusian man confronts "the absurd" and transcends it by his freedom."

However, at this point a sharp difference arises that marks the extent of divergence between a Christian existentialist like Merton and an atheist near-existentialist like Camus. For Camus, man's freedom and his power through that freedom to make himself — and hence to defy the absurdity of existence — gave the only solution to the human condition in a universe that was splendid but indifferent. For Merton the recognition of absurdity, the nausea at one's own human unworthiness, helped to lead one into the dark night where God, an absence in the Camusian universe, might choose to accept man's choice.

> The monk faces the worst and discovers in it the hope of the best. From the darkness comes light. From death, life. From the abyss there comes, unaccountably, the mysterious gift of the Spirit sent by God to make all things new, to transform the created and redeemed world, and to re-establish all things in Christ.

Hope is here the crucial concept. Camus rejected hope in much the same way as the Buddhist rejects desire, as a deception that prevents man from facing up to the reality of his condition, as a hankering that prevents him from accepting his destiny with dignity and gaining happiness from what cannot be changed. Merton, like Blake, accepted and praised desire, in the sense of the desire that leads man to search for God, and he laid so much stress on hope that he has at times been described as one of the creators of a contemporary theology of hope. He does indeed observe a close relationship between hope and freedom, as he stresses in that somewhat sententious collection of religious aphorisms, *No Man Is an Island*.

> We are not perfectly free until we live in pure hope. For when our hope is pure, it no longer trusts exclusively in human and visible means, nor rests in any visible end. He who hopes in God trusts God, Whom he never sees, to bring him to the possession of things that are beyond imagination.

But if one is to be an existentialist and also to trust in something beyond visible means and ends, one must believe that spiritual experience, the encounter with God, is an existential reality, a matter of actual being, and the only way one can believe that is by accepting mysticism, which Merton did. For him the contemplative life had no savour of idealism; it was a probe into reality, a quest into the very heart of existence.

But the meeting place of all existentialisms remains the wasteland or — to give it a name even more redolent of traditional meaning for the Judeo-Christian mind — the desert, and it is through the desert that we must go in search of the Merton who wore the other face to that of the cenobitic monk: Merton the eremitic contemplative.

From the beginning Merton was fascinated with the concept of the desert. So far as I know, he never saw a real desert until the last year of his life, when he twice visited the Benedictine Monastery of Christ in the Desert at Chama Canyon in New Mexico before his departure for Asia, but in both historic and symbolic terms the desert was immensely important to him. It was the place where the Israelites wandered and where Moses encountered God; the place where the Essenes formed their proto-monastic community and out of which John the Baptist emerged as the forerunner; the place where Christ was tempted. In the deserts of Egypt Christian monasticism first developed, and the Desert Fathers, the hermit saints of the fourth century AD, were the predecessors in solitary contemplation on whom Merton looked back with most affection. The most attractive of his early poems, "The Prophet," begins with the haunting lines:

> I met a traveller from the holy desert,
> Honeycomb, beggarbread eater,
> Lean from drinking rain
> That lies in the windprints of rocks.

As a symbol — and as a strongly visualized image in the narrower sense — the desert appears constantly in Merton's poems and also in his writings on the contemplative life. It takes on both the symbolic forms which he defines when discussing the Psalms in *Bread in the Wilderness* — the typological and the cosmic; it adds a third form, the mystical. The desert of the Old Testament typologically anticipates the desert of the New Testament, which in turn anticipates the desert where monasticism was founded and where the first hermit saints made their search for God. In cosmic terms the desert, like the sea and the mountain, is one of those forms in nature which have moved through the myths and the poetry of mankind since earliest times. The actual desert is full of elements that lend themselves to symbolic use; it is a place of marginal life, sparse and tenacious life; it is a place of hunger and thirst and heat and cold; a place where the rigours of nature are most ferociously experienced; a place where a man faces the perils of his own weaknesses; a place where brotherhood and hospitality are matters of life and death; a place where every day is a walking through the valley of death's shadow. In legendary terms it is the place where demons live, the place of testing and temptations, and hence the place of saintly victories and angelic encounters. And all these aspects are taken up into myth and applied to the religious life.

The monastery in figurative terms becomes a desert and the hermitage an even more rigorous one; the Christian life abounds in such simulations of the desert as Lent, which commemorates Christ's forty days of wilderness temptation; the spiritual path of man is seen as a pilgrimage through a desert where encounters diabolical or divine may take place. It is at this point that the symbolism of the desert passes from the cosmic and the typological into the mystical.

Images of the desert are scattered throughout Merton's poems, appearing in many of the works which I have called poems of the choir, but the true desert poems are a relatively small group of quite distinctive works which are characterized by spareness, control, short quiet lines, a laconic manner that bows towards silence. Some of them are about desert saints and fathers. One is about the Old Testament prophet Elias. "Dry Places" is about a man-made desert. And some — like "In Silence" — do not mention deserts at all, yet in spareness of form and feeling belong to the wilderness.

"Elias — Variations on a Theme" is perhaps the best of these desert poems. It is really a meditation on the nature of spiritual freedom. In manner it sometimes seems to echo T. S. Eliot: "The free man does not float / On the tides of his own expedition / Nor is he sent on ventures as busy men are, / Bound to an inexorable result," though when God appears to promise a rendezvous in solitude, he speaks rather like William Blake:

> *"Where the fields end*
> *Thou shalt be My friend.*
> *Where the bird is gone*
> *Thou shalt be My son."*

The opening verse of "Elias" is an excellent example of the clean laconism of Merton's desert style.

> Under the blunt pine
> In the winter sun
> The pathway dies
> And the wilds begin.
> Here the bird abides
> Where the ground is warm
> And sings alone.

After his life of restless questioning, his arguments with God, Elias comes to the solitude beyond intention. "The pathway dies, / The journey has begun." These are the images of the mystical quest, and they lead Elias towards the freedom which is that of birds and not of busy men. Here we come to a passage (in a collection published in 1949) which suggests that even at this stage, when he was reading mainly Christian religious writings, the Scriptures and the Fathers of the Church, the Scholastics and the Spanish mystics, Merton may already have begun his fruitful meeting of minds with Lao Tzu and Chuang Tzu, for what he says might well have be written by a Taoist poet (and perhaps also by a Blake writing in free verse):

> Here the bird abides
> And sings on top of the forgotten
> Storm. The ground is warm.
> He sings no particular message.
> His hymn has one pattern, no more planned,
> No less perfectly planned
> And no more arbitrary
> Than the pattern in the seed, the salt,
> The snow, the cell, the drop of rain.

But the free man is not only alone as birds are. "As above, so below," the hermetic sages insisted, and for Merton the free man also sings "as universes do. Built / On his own inscrutable pattern / Clear, unmistakable, not invented by himself alone / Or for himself, but for the universe also." It is a statement of existential freedom as impressive in its own God-centred way as any made by Camus or Sartre without benefit of deity, and the final lines of "Elias," in my view, are among the best poetry — and the most moving — that Merton ever wrote:

> Under the blunt pine
> Elias becomes his own geography
> (Supposing geography to be necessary at all),
> Elias becomes his own wild bird, with God in the center,
> His own wide field which nobody owns,
> His own pattern, surrounding the Spirit
> By which he is himself surrounded:
>
> For the free man's road has neither beginning nor end.

The free man is the solitary man: not the lonely man, but the man who has learned to find his sufficiency in solitude. This is why the early hermit fathers of the Egyptian desert appealed so strongly to Merton, and in a less romantic way than they appealed to Flaubert and Anatole France. He dedicated a whole book — and a very appealing one — to the hermits who lived in the desolate region known as the Scete, in northern Egypt, west of the Nile towards Libya. *The Wisdom of the Desert* consists largely of anecdotes about these simple and saintly men who, as Merton said, "had in fact become free by paying the price of freedom."

In their own age, the Desert Fathers had escaped from a decaying and materialistic society, an ugly metropolitan world — that of the declining Roman Empire, which in many ways was much like our own — and, as Merton longed to do, they found an alternative way of life in the desert, a marginal way, not of open rebellion but of splendid evasion.

> The flight of these men to the desert was neither purely negative nor purely individualistic. They were not rebels against society. True, they were in a certain sense "anarchists," and it will do no harm to think of them in that light. They were men who did not believe in letting themselves be passively guided and ruled by a decadent state, and who believed that there was a way of getting along without slavish dependence on accepted, conventional values.

They lived in charity to each other; despite their general asceticism, they were lavish in providing hospitality from their scanty means which they earned with the labour of their own hands, mainly basket weaving. They talked, as Merton remarks, little of God, "because they knew that when one has been somewhere close to His dwelling, silence makes more sense than a lot of words." They sought what Merton called *quies* or "rest," but they had little highfalutin talk about the contemplative life. They believed in acting freely in response to the inner voice. As one of them said: "Whatever you see your soul to desire according to God, do that thing, and you shall keep your heart safe." Humility, poverty and reluctance to judge or despise others were the great virtues in their eyes, and solitude was a sovereign master. "Go, sit in your cell," said the black hermit Moses, "and your cell will tell you everything." Most of them, as Merton remarks, "lived their lives out to a good old age among the rocks and sands" and "only did so because they had come into the desert to be themselves, their *ordinary* selves, and to forget a world that divided them from themselves."

The Desert Fathers were elaborate neither in their liturgies when they met together nor in the private prayers they conducted in their hermitages, yet in Merton's view the customs of these solitary men played a vital role in establishing the Christian monastic tradition. In *Contemplative Prayer* he discussed their meditations with great sympathy, and remarked that though they were often in fact mystics, they did not imagine themselves to be such, and that far from seeking extraordinary experiences they "contented themselves with the struggle for 'purity of heart' and for control of their thoughts, to keep their minds and hearts empty of care and concern, so that they might altogether forget themselves and apply themselves entirely to the love and service of God."

They expressed their love in a love of God's word, drawing their prayer from the Psalms, meditating on the Scriptures. But there was nothing analytical or intellectual about such exercises. "Meditation for them consisted in making the words of the Bible their own by memorizing them and repeating them, with deep and simple concentration, 'from the heart.' Therefore the 'heart' comes to play a central role in this primitive form of monastic prayer."

For Merton these early Desert Fathers embodied a pristine monastic simplicity that haunted him as a model and an ideal, and some of his best poems of the desert were written about the two hermits named Macarius, who were among his favourites.

In "Macarius the Younger" he evokes with an appropriately modest lucidity of language the relationship between the desert and those feel impelled to go there:

> No road, no path,
> No land marks
> Show the way there.
> You must go by the stars.
>
> Scarce is the water:
> Where found at all
> It smells poisonous as tar
> But is safe to drink.
>
> Few live there
> Far apart
> Out of one another's sight
> True men of God:
> Such a place
> Suffers only those
> Who have made up their minds.
>
> There is great love among them
> And love for any other
> Who can get that far.
> If any traveller
> Should reach that place
> He receives much care:
> One who crosses such wastes
> Has needs.

And so, the poet implies, does anyone who enters that condition of the soul which metaphorically we call the desert, that agony of existential dread out of which freedom can inexplicably emerge.

In the third part of the poem the two Macarii, "both men of God," decide to visit a brother hermit and take the ferry across the Nile, which is crowded with Roman officers and soldiers. One of the tribunes sees the hermits, "like a pair of sacks/ . . . ragged bums, having nothing, / Free men."

> "You" he said, "are the happy ones.
> You laugh at life. You need nothing from the world
> But a few rags, a crust of bread."

And one Macarius replied: "It is true,
We follow God. We laugh at life.
And we are sorry life laughs at you."

Then the officer saw himself as he was.
He gave away all that he had
And enlisted in the desert army.

There was nothing Merton wanted more than to enlist in the desert army, even though he recognized that his times and perhaps also his personal past made it difficult for him to live just as they lived; even deserts today are patrolled and those without proper papers are no longer allowed to inhabit their holes and caves. But the desert as a type of the modern hermitage still haunted him, and even when he gained his own hermitage in the woods of Gethsemani, with its partially solitary life, he was not entirely content with this refuge, which he uneasily felt had been given to him for the wrong reasons — because he was famous and needed to escape from his admirers — and he still toyed with the idea of finding remotenesses, in the deserts of the American southwest, in Alaska, in the California sierra, where he would be more truly removed from human society, more in tune with the natural world, nearer to his true and "ordinary" self, more vulnerable to God's love.

He thought deeply and even with a considerable degree of practicality about the achievement of the solitary life. In spite of the misgivings of his superiors, who were after all functionaries in an order dedicated to cenobitic monasticism, he believed that the hermitage was really a natural extension of monastic inclinations. "All monasticism is in some sense solitary and even the common life has its spiritual roots in eremitical solitude. The desert ideal is the monastic ideal as such, and the value of cenobitism is that it makes a certain solitude, austerity and renunciation of the world possible to the average man who would have no desire and no need to become a real hermit."

And if Merton believed that eremitic reclusion was really a necessary extension of monasticism, a pushing of outposts into the farther desert, he also believed that it was quite consistent with his priestly vocation. For to Merton what made the priest different from other men was not his pastoral role, his activities of teaching and advising other men or consoling and praying for them. It was not even that the priest is a man of God, for "The monk is a man of God and he does not have to be a priest." What distinguishes the priest is his sacramental role, his role as a "Visible human instrument of the Christ who reigns in Heaven," and this role is carried out when he re-enacts Christ's death and sacrifice in the mystery of the Mass.

> This explains at once the beauty and the terror of the priestly vocation. A man, weak as other men, imperfect as they are, perhaps less well endowed than many of those to whom he is sent, perhaps even less inclined to be virtuous than some of them, finds himself caught, without possibility of escape, between the infinite mercy of Christ and the almost infinite dreadfulness of man's sin. He cannot help but feel in the depths of his heart something of Christ's compassion for sinners, something of the eternal Father's hatred of sin, something of the inexpressible love that drives the Spirit of God to consume sin in the fires of sacrifice. At the same time he may feel in himself all the conflicts of human weakness and irresolution and dread, the anguish of uncertainty and helplessness and fear, the inescapable lure of passion. All that he hates in himself becomes more hateful to him, by reason of his close union with Christ. But also by reason of his very vocation he is forced to face resolutely the reality of sin in himself and in others. He is bound by his vocation to fight this enemy. He cannot avoid the battle. And it is a battle that he alone can never win. He is forced to let Christ Himself fight the enemy in him. He must do battle on the ground chosen not by himself but by Christ. That ground is the hill of Calvary and the Cross. For, to speak plainly, the priest makes no sense at all in the world except to perpetuate in it the sacrifice of the Cross, and to die with Christ on the Cross for the love of those whom God would have him save. (*No Man Is an Island*)

One is reminded here of the whisky priest in Graham Greene's *The Power and the Glory,* sinful and in terms of ordinary human standards despicable, yet heroic in his dedication to his sacramental role, to the extent that in the bitter end he sacrifices a certainty of freedom and becomes an unwilling martyr when he turns back into danger to give the last rites to a dying criminal. Yet the point that Merton would make in reconciling his priesthood with the eremitic life is perhaps a somewhat different one from Greene's; the dying criminal and the jungle pastorate are dispensible, and one can "keep alive the sacramental presence and action of the Risen Savior" even if one performs the Mass in the seclusion of a hermitage. Many Christians, even some Catholics, would not agree.

Convinced as Merton was of the value of the eremitic life, he was unsure how well that value could be sustained outside at least some kind of community, some kind of embracing and overriding discipline, and when he prepared a "Project for a Hermitage" (included in *The Monastic Journey*) for the attention of his Cistercian superiors, the Skete—or colony of scattered cells—that he envisioned had little of the looseness and informality of the fourth-century eremitic colonies in the Egyptian desert. The Skete would remain under the control of the monastery, with the permission both of the Abbot and of the Superior of the Skete being needed for any monk to become a hermit, and in everything—despite his God-given free will—the hermit would seek the approval of his Spiritual Father. In external terms, then, the hierarchical structure of the Order and of the Church would be preserved.

At this point, before passing on to the connections between Merton's idea of eremitic solitude and his view of the contemplative life, it is advisable to dwell a little more on his interpretations of the vow of obedience, since obedience necessarily implies authority, which is another way of describing that humanly corrupting thing called power, and in the present context we see authority extending itself into the ultimate solitudes of the religious life. Merton believed that for any deep involvement in the contemplative life, spiritual direction was a "moral necessity," and this was one of the points on which he would later find agreement with those Tibetan and Zen Buddhist teachers who insist on the need for gurus or masters to direct the neophyte's course. He distrusted any teaching, like that of the Quakers and other spiritually libertarian sects, which suggested that one might seek enlightenment unaided without incurring deep inner perils.

Merton in fact sustained a respect for ecclesiastical (as distinct from political) authority that—despite many strains and some evasions — lasted virtually unbroken to the end of his life. There is one passage in an essay on "The Solitary Life" published in Italy as late as 1960 which aroused my profound misgivings about Merton's view of obedience. Merton talks of the "virus of mendacity" which in modern times creeps into "every vein and organ of the social body," and he grants that it "would be abnormal and immoral if there were no reaction." Then he goes on:

> It is even healthy that the reaction should sometimes take the form of outspoken protest, as long as we remember that where Christian obedience is concerned, even manifest errors on the part of hierarchical authority are no justification for rebellion and disobedience, and the observations made by subjects should never be lacking in the respect due to Superiors, or in submission to authority as such. Solitude, in other words, is no refuge for the rebellious.

One may surely ask whether there is not a limit beyond which the "manifest errors on the part of hierarchical authority" become an intolerable tyranny and must be disobeyed. Certainly on this point the non-Christian existentialists are unanimously opposed to Merton's view. Perhaps they might not go as far as Oscar Wilde, who claimed that "Disobedience . . . is man's original virtue," but Camus in particular regarded rebellion as an essential element in man's self-definition in the face of an absurd destiny, and devoted a whole book, *The Rebel,* to proving his point.

And if obedience is held to be limitless, what are we to say to Thomas Merton, who wrote so splendidly on the case of that "obedient, loyal" man, faithful to authority, Adolf Eichmann? And what would Merton answer if we were to ask him of that other "obedient, loyal" man, faithful to authority, Tomas de Torquemada, the Grand Inquisitor, and those who obeyed him? How deeply did Merton ponder the meaning which Dostoevsky, whom he respected, meant us to distill from Ivan Karamazov's "Legend of the Grand Inquisitor"? It is true that Merton on several occasions condemned the excesses of the Inquisition, yet he never challenged obedience to ecclesiastical as he did obedience to lay authority.

Certainly, as we shall later see, Merton's obedience was to be greatly strained during the 1960s by his sense of the need for social criticism, for manifestations of solidarity with the disinherited, yet he never took the final step of openly defying constituted authority, and he parted from many Catholic radicals on this issue.

Yet the reasons behind Merton's attitude are evident. However widely he opened his mind in some directions during his later years, he remained a convinced traditionalist, carefully distinguishing tradition from convention. And he was, after all, an eschatologist as well as a mystic. He was one who looked to the Parousia, the resurrection in transfigured form of all creation, the remaking of the world, the coming of the City of God without as well as the Kingdom of God within, and he believed that in these events, which would happen literally and not figuratively, the visible Church, whose life "is the Truth of God Himself, breathed out into the Church by his Spirit," had its destined and necessary role. And so in the church militant there must be no breaking of ranks. The disciplines must be maintained. Obedience must continue.

Perhaps also Merton felt the need to reassure those concerned with ecclesiastical authority that—given its inevitable stress on the direct way—the contemplative life was not subersive of the mediational role of the Church, the apostolic pattern. At one point he reproaches some of the admirers of the Catholic mystics for believing "that these rare men somehow reached the summit of contemplation in defiance of Catholic dogma." And he adds: "But the truth is that the saints arrived at the deepest and most vital and also the most individual and personal knowledge of God precisely because of the Church's teaching authority, precisely through the tradition that is guarded and fostered by that authority."

In fact, as we well know, the St. John of the Cross whom Merton so much admired was imprisoned because of his differences with the ecclesiastical authorities, and another of the great mystics to whom he often refers, Meister Eckhart, one of the great forerunners of Christian existentialism, was harried to his death with charges of heresy and personally condemned by Pope John XXII. This, surely, is a curious way of guarding and fostering.

St. John, and even Meister Eckhart were later accepted by the Church. Miguel de Molinos, the seventeenth-century mystic, was not, and Merton is uncharacteristically shrill in his denunciation of the quietism of Molinos, which, like the infused contemplation Merton defended, also consisted of a waiting for God, though in the case of Molinos the waiting was completely passive and lacking in the alert seeking activated by the soul's free will that Merton talked of.

In such areas, as Evelyn Underhill remarked when she wrote of the Quietists, "the line between the true and false doctrine was a fine one," and it remains fine when one tries to draw the distinction between heretical quietism and a contemplative way as wedded to solitude and silence as Merton's. Even the phraseology of the last of the poems of the desert that I shall quote, "In Silence," might lead the reader who had not been alerted to Merton's disquisitions on the contemplative life to imagine that here in fact is a plea for at least a kind of quietism.

The poem evokes a place of stillness and silence beyond even the Trappist mingling of silence and work noise and psalmodic sound. It is the silence of a hermit's cell in which the soul is called to listen, and in which quietude — the *quies* of the Desert Fathers — becomes the way of knowing, through the voices of God's creatures living their ordained and particular lives, one's true self. Invoking The soul to "Be still / Listen to the stones of the wall / Be silent, they try / To speak your / Name," the poem asks:

> Who (be quiet)
> Are you (as these stones
> Are quiet). Do not
> Think of what you are
> Still less of
> What you may one day be.
> Rather
> Be what you are (but who?) be
> The unthinkable one
> You do not know.

And the soul answers that he will try to be his own silence but that this is difficult, because "The whole / World is secretly on fire."

> ". . . How can a man be still or
> Listen to all things burning? How can he dare
> To sit with them when
> All their silence
> Is on fire?"

That fire, we sense, is also God's dark light, and perhaps also the flames of the Paraclete that urge men to speak with tongues. "We enter into possession of God when he invades all our faculties with His light and His infinite fire." (*New Seeds of Contemplation*)

Merton wrote much on the contemplative life and the mystical way. By the nature of the subject, which does not lend itself to elaborate intellectual structures, the books he wrote could rarely be regarded as theological or philosophical treatises; he only wrote one book of this kind, early in his writing career. This was *Ascent to Truth* (1951); it was justly regarded as mediocre by theologians and boring by general readers, and Merton did not repeat the experiment.

It is true that *Contemplative Prayer,* which was first conceived as a manual for novice monks, has some of the sequential unity of a teaching text. But most of the books in which Merton treats of the contemplative life resemble his journals in being discontinuous and yet having a kind of cumulative development; they are mosaics related to the time of reading rather than to the space of looking. *No Man Is an Island* does not merely take its title from John Donne; the form, which is that of a number of unconnected yet related disquisitions on various aspects of the religious life, bears a strong resemblance to Donne's *Devotions,* in which, of course, occurs the maxim whose implications echo through all of Merton's writings: "No man is an Island, entire of itself; every man is a piece of the Continent, a part of the main." Books like *The New Man* (1961) and *Life and Holiness* (1963) are collections of brief homilies loosely gathered around a single thought, and *Seeds of Contemplation*—which eventually metamorphosed into the larger and much more mature *New Seeds of Contemplation*— is, as Merton himself described it, "a volume of more or less disconnected thoughts and ideas and aphorisms about the interior life."

Merton himself at this point draws attention to the fact that many of the great religious writers of the past, and particularly those of mystical rather than theological bent, were attracted towards this kind of presentation of their thoughts. He mentions, as part of "the long tradition of such writing," Pascal's *Pensées,* the *Cautelas* and *Avisos* of St. John of the Cross, the *Meditationes* of Guigo the Carthusian, "or, for that matter, *The Imitation of Christ.*" He might, of course, have added *The Cloud of Unknowing,* which was assembled—probably over years of contemplation—as a sequence of thoughts building up by association, and the *Talks of Instruction* of Meister Eckhart, "held with some of his spiritual children, who asked him about many things as they sat together at collation."

Merton refers to "the long tradition," and he was a traditionalist not merely in his loyal adherence for better or for worse to the Catholic Church but also in his attitude towards the contemplative search and towards its result, which is the mystical experience. To be just to Merton, one must emphasize that his view of tradition was in no sense a static one. When he contrasted tradition with convention in *No Man Is an Island,* he drew this out quite clearly.

> Tradition is living and active, but convention is passive and dead. Tradition does not form us automatically: we have to work to understand it. Convention is accepted passively, as a matter of routine. Therefore convention easily becomes an evasion of reality. It offers us only pretended ways of solving the problems of living — a system of gestures and formalities. Tradition really teaches us to live and shows us how to take full responsibility for our own lives. Thus tradition is often flatly opposed to what is ordinary, to what is mere routine. But convention, which is a mere repetition of familiar routines, follows the line of least resistance. . . .
>
> Finally, tradition is creative. Always original, it always opens out new horizons for an old journey. Convention, on the other hand, is completely unoriginal. It is slavish imitation. It is closed upon itself and leads to complete sterility.

In Merton's view the contemplative life, like tradition, was open-ended, a matter of ever new horizons, and hence it had no con-

nection with the conventional elements of the pious or pietistic
life.

The existence of a contemplative tradition is, of course, one
of the many apparent paradoxes that hover around the whole
subject of mysticism. In itself, the mystical experience is secret
and particular; it can only come to a person within his most private being and it is virtually uncommunicable except in metaphorical and virtually poetic terms. It seems the least likely of all
experiences to have been fitted into the life of a highly organized
Church obsessed with liturgy and at times at least partially corrupted by its political connections, and equally it seems the least
likely of all experiences to provide the content for a well defined
religious succession. Yet both these things happened, and the
mystical or contemplative tradition has proved one of the most
durable elements in Christianity—as it has, indeed, in Buddhism
and Hinduism and, though perhaps to a lesser extent, in Islam
and Judaism.

The mystical tradition is not merely far more widespread
than Christianity; it is also far more ancient, and elements of
the many mystery religions of the Hellenistic world found their
way into the primitive Church. There are strong mystical elements
in the Gospel according to St. John and in the teachings of St.
Paul, and these may have reached Christianity through the Essenes
of Palestine, through the contemplative communities which Philo
described in Alexandria round about the time of the Crucifixion,
and through the early Gnostic cults of the eastern Mediterranean.
The ideas and perhaps the practices of that pagan master contemplative, the neo-Platonist Plotinus, entered the Christian tradition
through the eclecticism of St. Augustine and of the mysterious
pseudo-Dionysius, the so-called Dionysius the Areopagite who pre-
tended to be a contemporary of Paul but actually wrote in the
fifth century and who—drawing on Plotinus and Philo, Porphyry
and Proclus, the last of the great pagan thinkers—established
within the Church the concept of the direct encounter with the
One, the All, God. Dionysius became in the middle ages an authority whose statements carried almost the weight of revealed writings,
and some of his central concepts, like that of the "Divine Dark,"
of the contemplative quest as a way of negation—a "divine ignor-

ance"—and of the necessary negation of all that the everyday consciousness perceives, recur in the writings of mystics and are repeated in the mid-twentieth century by Thomas Merton in only slightly varying forms.

Meanwhile, far away from the centres of growing political and ecclesiastical power, the Egyptian Desert Fathers were evolving the practical, earthy and distinctly unliterary kind of mysticism which Merton celebrates in *The Wisdom of the Desert*. They lived the holy life and found it necessary to talk little and write less about it; the most famous among them, St. Anthony, is generally thought to have been illiterate, and so undoubtedly were many of the others. But one of Merton's ragged Macarii—St. Macarius the Egyptian—taught in his homilies that by a combination of labour, ascetic discipline and meditation one could finally experience the divine presence, and that one could progress to continually greater spiritual attainment because the divine was infinite and therefore inexhaustible. John Cassian, who also figures prominently in Merton's writings on the contemplative path, travelled for seven years in the fourth century as a pilgrim among the Egyptian monasteries and hermitages, and returned to report in his *Dialogues* the conversations he had with the Desert Fathers on the nature and practice of contemplative prayer. Cassian's was a highly influential work in the history of early mediaeval monasticism, providing St. Benedict with many of the ideas which he incorporated into the Rule of the Benedictine order, the precursor of the Cistercians, when he founded it during the sixth century, in the depth of the dark ages.

In Merton's early pattern of reading there was a skip—if one makes an exception of Dante—from the Desert Fathers and St. Augustine, to the sixteenth-century Spanish mystics: to Ignatius Loyola, whose *Spiritual Exercises* he read with relatively little edification during the early days of his conversion, and to the great Carmelite contemplatives, St. Teresa and St. John of the Cross, whose eloquent descriptions of the ecstatic state, so psychologically true and at the same time so metaphorically evocative, appealed throughout Merton's life to the poet in him as well as to the contemplative monk.

During his period as Master of Scholastics, Merton was much

involved with such theological teachers as St. Thomas Aquinas, whose theory of infused contemplation (in which God searches out the willing soul) he adopted, and at the same time he discovered the great mystics of the Rhineland: Meister Eckhart, with his daring, drastic and proto-existentialist descriptions of "the desert of the Godhead where no one is at home"; the gentle and humane John Tauler of Strasburg, and the Fleming, Ruysbroeck.

Finally, knowing already the late flowering of the tradition in the poems and prophetic books of William Blake, he came to the small school of English mystics of the fourteenth century: Walter Hilton, the hermit Richard Rolle, the anchoress Julian of Norwich, and the anonymous and learned village priest who wrote *The Cloud of Unknowing*. They were modest and saintly people, exemplary in their self-effacement, though Rolle from his hermitage would on occasion denounce the evils of contemporary religious and secular life with a courage that led the Lollards to accept him as a predecessor. *The Cloud of Unknowing,* which introduced English contemplatives to Dionysius the Areopagite, is a work of singular grace, literary as well as spiritual, and Julian of Norwich's *Revelations of Divine Love* is one of the most truly poetic of all mystical writings, as Merton lovingly recognized.

In this tradition which fed him, Merton will undoubtedly have his place by virtue of experience and eloquent exposition. But of what does the tradition in fact consist? It is not in the strict sense a historical tradition, for unlike the theological structure, the mystical insight is not affected by such accidents as our changing knowledge of the universe, and hence Merton could disregard both the orthodox mediaeval cosmology that Thomism accepted and also the changing astronomies that have superseded it when he said: "Our discovery of God is, in a way, God's discovery of us. We cannot go to Heaven to find Him because we have no way of knowing where Heaven is or what it is." (*New Seeds of Contemplation*)

The mystical tradition continues regardless of theologies (traditional or new) and equally regardless of innovative sciences.

Nor is the mystical tradition carried on by the secret transmission of esoteric formulae that are whispered in the ear in the manner of Tibetan gurus, or indeed by any kind of actual teaching. As Merton remarks, in spite of all his talk of Spiritual Directors, "as soon as you think of yourself as teaching contemplation to others, you make another mistake. No one teaches contemplation except God, Who gives it. The best you can do is write something or say something that will serve as an occasion for someone else to realize what God wants of him." (*New Seeds*)

One may perhaps draw an analogy from the teaching of the arts. Creative writing courses are usually dismal failures in which even good poets strive in vain to transmit their personal insights or to stir creative powers in others. This is because they proceed according to method; they teach techniques and provide informed criticism. But once in a generation there appears a poet who by some special charisma is able to stimulate the creativity of others. I have encountered precisely two cases in almost fifty years in the craft, one within the classroom and one outside. Forty years ago, by the sheer power and luminosity of his writing, W. H. Auden propagated his insights to many younger English poets and founded a genuine innovatory movement. Theodore Roethke's inspiration was personal and direct, and I remember very vividly his conducting a poetry writing course at Seattle twenty years ago in which an amazing number of people reached under his charismatic spell the knowledge that poetry was their vocation.

I can imagine that—while most self-styled "meditation teachers" are either charlatans or self-deluded people—some of the great mystics could indeed transmit a vocation to others in a similar charismatic way, as Elijah transmitted a vocation to Elisha, but that is not the same as the kind of teaching tradition by which the Dominicans sustained for so long the ascendancy of Thomist theology in the Catholic Church. However, it seems evident that Merton himself had no access to any such charismatic master, as would probably be true of most of the great contemplatives who have appeared since the seventeenth century.

What have sustained the tradition are in fact—despite the contempt for literary expression which many mystics have expressed—a succession of written documents and an inherited pattern of metaphors, together with some basic techniques for initiating the contemplative process.

The mystical encounter is direct, personal and particular;

there is no mediator, since the Spiritual Director—where one exists—can merely give advice on the path. As it is an experience neither physical nor intellectual, the possibility of describing it in scientific terms or even in terms of ordinary literary narrative does not exist. At best one can suggest it by the use of appropriate metaphor, and ever since the days of the pseudo-Dionysius a virtual figurative code has existed, refined and expanded over the generations, by which, through metaphors of light and darkness, of skies and seas, of suns and space, etc., the mystics have been able over the centuries to recognize the similarity of their experiences.

This literary heritage, which in the work of contemplatives like St. John of the Cross and Julian of Norwich and William Blake embraces some of the finest of religious poetry, is one of the ways in which a mystical tradition has been sustained. The other way is that of inherited techniques. These do not resemble the mechanical techniques of yoga, which are based on formulae aimed at the establishment of self-control in order to develop occult powers. The destination of the true mystic is not power, whose deceptions he has long recognized, but union with God, and the best that can be achieved by the inherited techniques, embodied in scores of meditational handbooks of which *The Imitation of Christ* is only the most famous, is an indication of how the aspirant can best arrange his mind for the contemplative journey. Such books cannot implant or even inspire the mystical experience; at best they can arouse the will to pursue it. Thus even Merton's *Contemplative Prayer,* which is one of the best books of its kind, turns out in the end to be little more than an attempt to define the contemplative life, to tell a little of the history of Christian mysticism, and to warn members of monastic communities of the pitfalls they may encounter. The one book on the mystical path that can be included among Merton's major works, and that has been called a "spiritual classic," succeeds precisely because its strategy is one of masterly indirection. Its scope embraces not only the contemplative and his special vocation but also his relationship to the temporal and physical world in which he continues to exist at the same time as he exists in the timeless world of the spirit. This is *New Seeds of Contemplation.*

As its title suggests, *New Seeds* had predecessors. *Seeds of*

Contemplation was written in 1948, some time before Merton's ordination, and published in 1949; after the success of *The Seven Storey Mountain,* it sold unexpectedly well, particularly among Catholics, and somewhat later in the same year a revised version appeared. Thirteen years elapsed before *New Seeds* appeared, and this contained so much new material (about a third of the book in length) and so many modifications of the text, that it was more than a mere revision; hence the title's suggestion of fresh insights. *New Seeds* was in fact the work of a changed author with a changed view of his subject and of the world.

The Merton who wrote *Seeds of Contemplation* was still the zealous young monk of *The Seven Storey Mountain;* his spiritual inclinations had perhaps intensified, but his ideas had certainly narrowed down during eight years of fairly strict reclusion when his contact with the outside world was so slight that he did not even have access to newspapers. As he said in 1948, in his original Author's Note, "This is the kind of book that writes itself almost automatically in a monastery." In 1962 he commented that *Seeds of Contemplation* had been originally written "in a kind of isolation, in which the author was alone with his own experience of the contemplative life." *New Seeds,* he added, had also been *written* in solitude, but "the author's solitude has been modified by contact with other solitudes; with the loneliness, the simplicity, the perplexity of novices and scholastics of his monastic community; with the loneliness of people outside any monastery; with the loneliness of people outside the Church."

During the intervening period Merton had read widely again after a period of almost exclusively Catholic reading; he had rediscovered the oriental sages, had discovered Protestant theologians and atheist existentialists, had opened a wide correspondence with people of many viewpoints and vocations. In *Seeds* he had been anxious to insist that he departed in no way from "Christian tradition," and there seems little doubt that he had mainly in mind a Catholic readership. In the next decade or so he seems to have become aware that there were many Catholics, even in the priesthood, who did not share his contemplative vocation or his desire for it, and at the same time to have realized that what he was offering might have a relevance that went beyond the Church and brought him into a fruitful contact with people of other ways of thought. This realization he made clear in the Preface to *New Seeds* where he declared that his book is meant only for "the few," perhaps not Stendhal's "Happy Few" but doubtless overlapping them:

> There are very many religious people who have no need for a book like this, because theirs is a different kind of spirituality. If to them this book is without meaning, they should not feel concerned. On the other hand, there are perhaps people without formal religious affiliations who will find in these pages something that appeals to them. If they do, I am glad, as I feel myself a debtor to them more than to the others.

Here we have Merton already opening his sympathies towards the broad inter-religious and inter-philosophical statements of his later years. Whom he means by the people without formal religious affiliations to whom he feels himself "a debtor more than to the others" is not at all clear, but he was certainly already in touch with Daisetz Suzuki, the Zen master, he was certainly reading Camus and Sartre, and he felt that he owed a great deal to people in the literary world and particularly to his agent Naomi Burton and to James Laughlin, who ran the avant-garde publishing house of New Directions and who brought out the books he valued most, including *New Seeds of Contemplation.*

Detailed comparisons between *New Seeds* and the two versions of *Seeds of Contemplation* have already been made (Donald Grayston, "Nova in Novis: The New Material in Thomas Merton's New Seeds of Contemplation," *Cistercian Studies,* Nos. 3 & 4, 1975) and I do not think it is necessary for me to repeat them here, since in a general study of this kind one is probably best advised to accept an author's own final judgement and take the last version he authorized of any of his works. I shall content myself with saying that in content and in viewpoint the new version is greatly broadened, and that in tone it is considerably less dogmatic and intolerant. I shall devote the rest of my brief comments to the significant aspects of its form and content.

New Seeds is, to begin, one of the most limpid of Merton's books: stylistically simple, completely lacking in rancour, and not without humour. The form — an intermingling of notes, personal reflections and aphorisms — gives a steady variation of texture so that one's mental focus is constantly and rather restfully shifted. This, I think, is a merit in a book that is not a sequentially ordered theological treatise, nor in any practical sense a meditational handbook, but rather a series of reflections whose aim is to establish an empathic understanding of the inexplicable, rather than to elicit intellectual agreement.

By this I do not mean that the book is without rational content. Far from it. There are chapters which can only be regarded as apologetic in character: for example, "The Woman Clothed with the Sun," a justification of the special role which the Virgin Mary holds in the eyes of Catholics and one that proceeds with a great deal of logical clarity once one accepts as a premise the reality of the Incarnation. If one does not, at least one is more aware of the reason for a devotion one does not share. And some of the aphorisms which stud the book are brilliant and often poetic summations of religious or moral truths.

> He is the "Thou" before whom our inmost "I" springs into awareness. He is the I AM before whom with our own most personal and inalienable voice we echo "I am."

> The "marriage" of body and soul in one person is one of the things that makes man the image of God: and what God has joined no man can separate without danger to his sanity.

> God utters me like a word containing a partial thought of himself. A word will never be able to comprehend the voice that utters it.

> When a proud man thinks he is humble his case is hopeless.

> Go into the desert not to escape other men but in order to find them in God.

> Love is my true identity. Selflessness is my true self. Love is my true character. Love is my name.

Blake, one feels, would not have despised such sayings.

After reading *New Seeds of Contemplation* several times I find in my religious unattachment that the more theological passages, passages in which Merton seeks to justify authority and dogma in the Church, are those which seem most intellectually indigestible and in which, despite their good Thomist reasoning, a degree of obstinate defensiveness survives, whereas the chapters which bring us towards the contemplative experience are wholly convincing and can be accepted outside reason—from the heart, as it were—as projections of experiential truth. These, I think, are the parts of the book in which the non-affiliated will, as Merton hopes, find "something that appeals to them," though in other parts of the book also there are points where Merton, in laying down the moral view of life and of the world that is a prerequisite for the contemplative quest, reflects the preoccupations of concerned people and even of activists who do not follow his special religious bent.

There are, for example, the passages in which he discusses with considerable psychological acuity the relationship between war and our irrational fears of our fellow men, and the passages on such questions as property which show him standing very close not only to the Christian radicals of the *Catholic Worker,* with whom in those years he developed a sympathetic contact, but also to libertarian critics of capitalism like Pierre-Joseph Proudhon or, in the American tradition, Josiah Warren:

> A man cannot be a perfect Christian—that is, a saint—unless he is also a communist. This means that he must either absolutely give up all right to possess anything at all, or else only use what he himself needs, of the goods that belong to him, and administer the rest for other men and for the poor: and in his determination of what he needs he must be governed to a great extent by the gravity of the needs of others. . . .
>
> If Christians had lived up to the Church's teaching about property and poverty there would never have been any occasion for the spurious communism of the Marxists and all the rest—whose communism starts out by denying *other men* the right to own property.

As a monk, of course, Merton was a practising communist, surrendering a considerable income in royalties to the monastic community and living an austere physical life; this gives a special pungency to his exhortation to the presumably non-monastic reader:

It is easy enough to tell the poor to accept their poverty as God's will when you yourself have warm clothes and plenty of food and medical care and a roof over your head and no worry about the rent. But if you want them to believe you — try to share some of their poverty and see if you can accept it as God's will yourself!

As we have already seen, one of the preoccupations which Merton shared with many contemporary Christian and secular thinkers was the alienation of man from his true self. Marx recognized the phenomenon, but blamed the capitalist system. Merton saw the cause in a spiritual malaise that could be cured only by man's reunion with the divine spirit, and for him this meant a journey into the inner self where the encounter with God that made man whole as a person, that made him a "new man," would ensue. There is a great deal in common between such a concept and Jung's idea of the process of individuation. "Individuation," said Jung in *Two Essays on Analytical Psychology*, "means becoming a single, homogenous being and, in so far as 'in-dividuality' embraces our innermost, last, and incomparable uniqueness, it also implies becoming one's own self. We could therefore translate individuation as 'coming to selfhood' or 'self-realization.' " The relationship between Merton's ideas and Jung's becomes all the more interesting when we realize that Jung regarded the "God-image" as an archetype of psychic wholeness and when we consider — in relation to Merton's discussions of the mystical experience — this passage from *Psychology and Alchemy:*

> It would be blasphemy to assert that God can manifest Himself everywhere save only in the human soul. Indeed the very intimacy of the relationship between God and the soul automatically precludes any devaluation of the latter. It would be going perhaps too far to speak of an affinity; but at all events the soul must contain in itself the faculty of relation to God, i.e. a correspondence, otherwise a connection could never come about. This correspondence is, in psychological terms, the archetype of the God-image.

Merton had certainly read the works of various psychoanalysts by the time he wrote *New Seeds of Contemplation,* for he recommended them as representing a field of study that Catholic theologians should not neglect. He even, in *New Seeds,* developed a kind of inner map of man not unlike that adumbrated by the psychoanalysts. He begins with a theological point:

> Faith, then, is the only way of opening up the true depths of reality, even of our own reality. Until a man yields himself to God in the consent of total belief, he must inevitably remain a stranger to himself, an exile from himself, because he is excluded from the most meaningful depths of his own being: those which remain obscure and unknown because they are too simple and too deep to be attained by reason.

Merton remarks that he does not mean by these depths the *subconscious,* which is only one aspect of the *unconscious* by which the "conscious mind of man is *exceeded in all directions*," and he makes "the important distinction between the animal, emotional and instinctive components of our unconscious and the spiritual, one might almost say 'the divine,' elements in our superconscious mind."

We have to accept the subconscious and come to terms with our animal nature, but it is in the superconscious that man's spiritual being, "which remains a pure mystery to his reason," exists and that God is present. Merton relates this triple division of the person to the traditional theology of the Greek fathers which used the terminology of Anima, Animus and Spiritus or Pneuma (significantly enough adopted by Jung also), and suggests that when the three are rightly ordered, "then man is reconstituted in the image of the Holy Trinity." One can draw at least an analogical comparison between this scheme and Freud's pattern of id, ego and superego, with the vital difference, of course, that Freud left no place in his scheme for God. Nor would Freud have agreed—or Jung for that matter—that faith is the *only* way of opening "the true depths . . . of our own reality."

One of Merton's most pressing concerns in writing *New Seeds* was to define "contemplation," a word which, like meditation, has in recent years been used to cover a wide variety of experiences and practices. This concern stayed with him to the end, and probably grew as he observed during the 1960s the spread of cultist movements offering meditational methods of varying authenticity. In *Contemplative Prayer,* his last work on the subject, he insisted that "True contemplation is not a psychological trick but a theological grace," and he went on to point out, as he had already done in *New Seeds,* the insufficiency and ambiguity of the term "contemplation" when applied to "the highest forms of Christian prayer." He warned against contemplation becoming the vehicle of "a kind of gnosticism which would elevate the contemplative above the ordinary Christian by initiating him into a realm of esoteric knowledge and experience, delivering him from the ordinary struggles and sufferings of human existence, and elevating him to a privileged state among the spiritually pure, as if he were almost an angel, untouched by matter and passion, and no longer familiar with the economy of sacraments, charity and the Cross." In *New Seeds* he had already added two new chapters entitled "What is Contemplation?" and "What Contemplation is Not" in which he emphasized that it is not a matter of visions, or of trances, or of occult powers, or of what are commonly called psychic phenomena, or of the exaltations to which the pious are often subject, or of mere pensiveness, and still less of the mental vacancy which some "meditational" techniques seek to induce. It *is* "a sudden gift of awareness, an awakening to the Real within all that is real. A vivid awareness of infinite Being at the roots of our own limited being." It is also "the response to a call . . . from Him Who has no voice" and an echo of God. "It is as if in creating us God asked a question, and in awakening us to contemplation He answered the question, so that the contemplative is at the same time, question and answer."

All this is, of course, metaphor, and on the surface all writing about mystical experience is metaphorical, which is why the best accounts are written not by theologians but by poets, whose power lies in penetrating to a deeper reality by abandoning the literalness of appearance and yet using its suggestive power. For, as Merton says, "The poet enters into himself in order to create. The contemplative enters into God in order to be created." And if the poet is also the contemplative who has gone through that process of creation, then the self into which he enters should inspire him with as pure an expression of his experience as words will allow. And this is the case as Merton tells of the deserts of aridity and the dark night of emptiness through which the contemplative often passes, and the "utter simplicity and obviousness of the infused light" that is finally given. This he does in terms that are not at all original — for the tradition of mystical symbolism is already established and he follows it — but with a clarity that strikes resonances in other contemplative and other poetic minds.

At God's touch, which is emptiness and empties the soul,

> A door opens in the center of our being and we seem to fall through it into immense depths which, although they are infinite, are all accessible to us; all eternity seems to have become ours in this one placid and breathless contact. . . .
>
> You seem to be the same person and you are the same person that you have always been: in fact you are more yourself than you have ever been before. You have only just begun to exist. You feel as if you were at last fully born. . . . You have sunk to the center of your own poverty, and there you have felt the doors fly open into infinite freedom, into a wealth which is perfect because none of it is yours and yet it all belongs to you.
>
> And now you are free to go in and out of infinity.
>
> It is useless to think of fathoming the depths of wide-open darkness that have yawned inside you, full of liberty and exultation.
>
> They are not a place, not an extent, they are a huge, smooth activity. These depths, they are Love. And in the midst of you they form a wide, impregnable country.

And that wide, impregnable country, with its starless night, that dark and singing desert, is, as Merton would find, the analogue to the luminous Void of the Buddhists, and perhaps more than an analogue, just as his God remarkably resembles the God of the Sufi who said: "I thought it was I who desired him, but no, it was He who desired me." The Hound of Heaven, Merton was learning, hunts in no single forest.

5

The World of Vatican II

At the end of 1958 the face and destiny of the Catholic Church were transformed by the election of Angelo Roncalli to be Pope John XXIII. The last Pope John, back in the fourteenth century, had connived at the persecution of Meister Eckhart for statements that seemed dangerous to Catholic orthodoxy, but the twentieth-century Pope John set an unprecedented example of tolerance and openness to change. He was a historian rather than a theologian, and he had the broad, sweeping view of human existence that characterizes the better kind of historical scholarship. He recognized that the defensive measures which the counter-Reformation Church had taken at the mid-sixteenth-century Council of Trent had the eventual effect of deep-freezing the Church into an exclusiveness and a doctrinal rigidity which made it appear a half-mediaeval, half-baroque institution that was fast becoming an anachronism in the rapidly changing world of the twentieth century.

The 77-year-old John—whom the cardinals had put in as a compromise caretaker Pope—surprised the conservative curia by revealing himself an active liberal in matters of Church policy and organization, though he was conservative in matters of ritual. The salient features of his pontifical reign can be summed up in two words that were always on his lips: *aggiornamento,* or bringing up to date, and *convivienza,* or living together. The Church had to adapt itself to the times it lived in by abandoning attitudes and practices that were obsolete and had no bearing on the fundamental and immutable truths of Christianity. And Catholics had to recognize that they lived in a world where there were other Christians and where there were non-Christian faiths that might embody true insights. Hence there should be a reconciliation among those whom history had divided. Without attempting to absorb them, the Church should recognize the "separated brethren" and should open a dialogue with them in this late and critical hour in man's history.

In one encyclical after the other, Pope John not merely preached change and dialogue but also called on Christians to recognize their social and political responsibilities in a world where the initiatives could not be left entirely in the hands of dictators or even of democratic political leaders. For the first time in the history of the papacy he also proclaimed the necessity for total liberty of belief and religious practice. In the encyclical *Pacem in Terris* he went against papal tradition by declaring that every human being should be allowed "to worship God in accordance with the right dictates of his own conscience, and to profess his religion both in private and in public."

Pope John further declared that "Truth calls for the elimination of every trace of racial discrimination," since "no man can be by nature superior to his fellows, since all men are equally noble in natural dignity." He insisted on removing from the Catholic liturgy traditional phrases that smelled of lingering anti-Semitism. While maintaining that as a philosophy Communism was false, he recognized that aspects of it were valid, and that a way of coexistence with Communist states must be discovered if the alternative were not to be a war he regarded as unthinkable. Therefore he called on all Catholics to work for disarmament and he stressed the need for those in the rich countries to ensure that the poor countries of the Third World be given the means to develop in freedom their characteristic ways of life.

At the historic Second Vatican Council, which opened in 1962 and continued after John's death in mid-1963, history was made by the presence of brotherly observers from Christian communities as varied as the ancient Coptic Church of Egypt and the Russian Orthodox Church in exile, the Nestorians of Ethiopia and the Monophysites of Armenia, the Anglicans and the Old Catholics, the Lutherans and the Quakers. Though they were not official delegates, the presence of the "separated brethren" strengthened the influence of the liberal bishops against the more conservative cardinals and their allies, and when Pope John raised his voice in support of doctrinal flexibility the result was that the key resolutions on the subject of Church authority and revelation deposed the Tridentine view of the authority of the Church being a source of revelation equal to that of the Scriptures. The *schemata* adopted by the Council were ecumenical in spirit and designed to be conciliatory to other Christian bodies.

The eventual result of the Council, commonly known as Vatican II, has been a series of radical changes in the Catholic Church involving not only the liturgy and such matters as monastic disciplines, which have dramatically relaxed over the past two decades, but also the internal functioning of the Church as a highly structured ecclesiastical organization. The authority of the bishops has been eroded, clergy and members of religious orders have defied their superiors and even broken their vows to return to the unconsecrated world, the opinions of lay Catholics on Church policy have been voiced more strongly than ever before, and the world is treated to the unaccustomed spectacle of bitter public debate among Catholics, particularly on such subjects as contraception and the marriage of priests. Democracy has found its way into an organization that traditionally was hierarchical and authoritarian, and the results — if not cataclysmic — have been drastic. The number of practising Catholics has declined rapidly, and the Church has lost much of the political influence it wielded in countries where it once allied itself with conservative parties and movements. Moreover, society as a whole has become increasingly secular, so that, as Merton remarked, "The Church is now in a world that is culturally 'post-Christian.'"

The Merton who saw these changes and who became an admirer and a supporter of Pope John, of *aggiornamento* and of *convivienza,* was so different a person from the young bigot who wrote *The Seven Storey Mountain* that one has to mark a second turning point in his life, round about 1957, and give it equal importance to his conversion in 1938. It is probably fruitless to speculate on the influence of Vatican II. Only the fact that many Catholics were already changing their attitude towards conservative and divisive traditions made feasible the reforms that Vatican II initiated under the guidance of Pope John, and Merton was one of those whose standpoint altered dramatically in the years before the Council. As a convert his attitude had been essentially Triumphalist, dominated by a baroque view of Catholicism that had ruled the Church for four centuries since the Council of Trent; it was an attitude encouraged by the sensational but fleeting period of monastic growth immediately after World War II when the Trappists doubled their numbers in the United States alone. But by the 1960s he had become reconciled to the possibility of a "diaspora" in which established churches might collapse and the few remaining dedicated Christians would be concerned with establishing the identity of their essential truths rather than with emphasizing the differences between their respective traditional myths.

It is obvious that one of the reasons why Merton's attitudes and activities changed so markedly round about the mid-1950s was the impossibility of a naturally curious and explorative mind remaining content with the narrow field of interests — the monastic experience, the joys and techniques of the contemplative life, the erudite study of the Church Fathers and the mediaeval mystics — that occupied him for more than a decade after his entry into the Abbey. There were external changes as well, within the Abbey and also in Merton's own circumstances, that encouraged him to turn his gaze outward and to open his mind in directions towards which for many years it had remained virtually closed. The stern Abbot of his early days at Gethsemani, Dom Frederic Dunne, who had been for fifty years a Trappist, maintained a discipline, in the tradition of de Rancé, so strict that Merton did not hear of the explosion of the nuclear bomb over Hiroshima until several months after it had taken place. When Dom Frederic died in 1948 — alone on a journey like Merton himself — his successor, Dom James Fox, began a series of gradual changes designed to take the Abbey back towards the world it had once so carefully excluded.

That world returned to Merton in human terms when he became Master of Novices in 1955; he retained that position for a decade, and this was a period when the youth of America was becoming deeply troubled with social and moral issues of unprecedented magnitude, exemplified in the civil rights campaign and in the tortuous questions raised by American intervention in the Vietnam war. It was inevitable that Merton, as their teacher and spiritual director, should find himself drawn into the mental and spiritual predicaments of the young men who were his charges, for by no means all the novices were deeply committed zealots who would remain in the Order; many were at Gethsemani because the problems and passions of that time of youth awakening and youth protest were hard for them to sort out or even to endure.

The realization that a withdrawal into solitude could not be valid if it implied separation from one's fellow men was brought dramatically home to Merton on a day in 1957 when he made one of his rare visits to Louisville. What he experienced then had an epiphanic quality which can only be appreciated by quoting at some length the relevant passage from the journal of thoughts and observations, *Conjectures of a Guilty Bystander,* which he kept at this time and which he insisted should not be regarded as a "spiritual journal" like *The Sign of Jonas.*

> In Louisville, at the corner of Fourth and Walnut, in the center of the shopping district, I was suddenly overwhelmed with the realization that I loved all those people, that they were mine and I theirs, that we could not be alien to one another even though we were total strangers. It was like waking from a dream of separateness, of spurious self-isolation in a special world, the world of renunciation and supposed holiness. The whole illusion of a separate holy existence is a dream. Not that I question the reality of my vocation, or of my monastic life: but the conception of "separation from the world" that we have in the monastery too easily presents itself as a complete illusion: the illusion that by making vows we become a different species of being, pseudoangels, "spiritual men," men of interior life, what have you. . . .

This sense of liberation from an illusory difference was such a relief and such a joy to me that I almost laughed out loud. And I suppose my happiness could have taken form in the words: "Thank God, thank God that I *am* like other men, that I am only a man among others." To think that for sixteen or seventeen years I have been taking seriously this pure illusion that is implicit in so much of our monastic thinking.

He goes on to talk of the "glorious destiny" it is to be "a member of the human race," of "the immense joy of being *man,* a member of a race in which God Himself became incarnate." And he ends in an epiphanic climax: "There is no way of telling people that they are all walking around shining like the sun."

From this point Merton saw himself, by virtue of his monastic status, as the quintessential "guilty bystander" of his title who is bound by his vocation not to be active in the world but bound also to be concerned, to bear his share of responsibility, and bound eventually, by his other vocation of writer, to recognize his involvement in the affairs of a world in crisis. As he would say a few years later, in 1966 in the Catholic journal *Commonweal:* "That I should have been born in 1915, that I should be the contemporary of Auschwitz, Hiroshima, Viet Nam and the Watts riots, are things about which I was not first consulted. Yet they are also events in which, whether I like it or not, I am deeply and personally involved."

When Merton began to turn away from his more conventionally religious writing in the period between 1941 and the mid-1950s, he did not really assume new preoccupations; rather, there was a resurrection of themes from the pre-conversion life which he had abandoned when he entered the Catholic Church. He began to re-examine the Protestantism which years before he had so contemptuously rejected, and to move on from dissenting believers to nonbelievers like the atheist existentialists. He took up, under another banner, the fight for social justice he had begun as a temporary Communist in the 1930s, and rediscovered the compassion for the disinherited that had once made him think of joining Catherine de Hueck Doherty in Harlem. To express his rising social militancy he turned in his poetry — as he had done in his pre-conversion fiction — to experimental forms and to the anti-poetry of indignation, and began to translate the poetry of the Third World. And in searching for answers to his spiritual questions he resumed on a deeper level the enquiry into Asian religions, and especially into Buddhism and Taoism, that he already embarked on in his student days.

Not merely was there a remarkable broadening in the range of Merton's writing and the scope of his reading during the last twelve years of his life; there was also a marked change in his manner of writing, a sharpening and a strengthening. His books tended even more than in the past to be mosaics, now not so much out of a preference for such discontinuous forms as because he was writing a great deal for periodicals of various kinds and he tended to make books out of groups of essays whose subjects were in a general way related.

Like his earlier journals and like the later *Asian Journal,* *Conjectures of a Guilty Bystander* (1966) is really the key book of this period, and in many ways it is the best work Merton produced in the years when he was at last looking from the monastic enclosure outward at the world rather than from the monastic enclosure inward at the self, as he did in *The Sign of Jonas.* I am not suggesting that the inner self is neglected in *Conjectures,* but the concern is less acute and urgent, and this may be a sign of the achievement of a degree of spiritual equilibrium that allows a diminution of self-consciousness and a broader view of the world at large. "I am less and less aware of myself simply as this individual who is a monk and a writer, and who, as monk and writer, sees this or writes that. It is my task to see and speak for many, when I seem to be speaking only for myself." The *many* must be interpreted widely, for the writing of this period is not only less didactic in its religious preoccupations than the works of Merton's early monastic years but also much more accessible to a readership increasingly composed of non-Catholics and even nonbelievers.

This change in Merton's approach, made all the easier by the progressive relaxation of the ecclesiastical censorship during these years, was accompanied by a much more direct, concrete and compact form of writing — less exalted, more earthy — in which the power of personal conviction exercised on crucial contemporary issues has largely replaced a reliance on accepted dogma.

Even the descriptive passages, which show Merton's continuing responsiveness to the beauties of the physical world, are more immediate in impact and less self-conscious in presentation than in the past. For example:

> Hawk. First the shadow flying downward along the wall of sunlit foliage. Then the bird itself, trim, compact substance, in the sky overhead, quite distinct from woods and trees, flying in freedom. Barred tail, speckled wings, with sunlight shining through them. He cut a half circle in emptiness over the elm. Then he seemed to put his hands in his pockets and sped, without a wing beat, like a bullet, to plunge into the grove across the open field.

Merton welcomed the forcefulness of Pope John XXIII's statements about world peace, and about "providence leading us to a new order in human relations." He praised the Pope's "spirit of openness and dialogue," and said that John shows "not only the greatness and simplicity of a truly Christian view of man, but also the living reality of the Christian and European tradition in culture." He saw the very act of calling the Second Vatican Council as important because it gave importance to the bishops rather than the papal curia and thus revived in men's minds a sense of "the diversity-in-unity of the universal Church, which is not simply a corporation with a head office in Rome." Already, in *Life and Holiness,* he had made his decentralist plea for the assertion of individual initiative within the Church: "There is no virtue in inertia or in a respondent and passive 'prudence' which refuses to move until the whole Church, from the Papal Curia on down, moves first."

Perhaps it was a sense of having found at last his own equilibrium in the monastic world that made Merton so willing at this time to seek common ground among the divided Christians. He found in himself no inclination to be anything but Catholic. "I believe in the Church," he says in *Conjectures.* "I am in a place where Christ has put me. Amen." Yet for the first time in his life he was able to speak out plainly — and to many audiences — against the defensive rigidities that, during the Tridentine centuries, had marred the Church.

He called the Church's opposition to experimental science "a great scandal and shame"; he agreed with Gandhi in accusing those who thought they possessed "absolute truth" of being offenders against brotherhood; he reminded his readers that the Christian faith "is a principle of questioning and struggle before it becomes a principle of certitude and of peace" and that "a moral code does not suppress choice, but educates and forms liberty." And he argued that the acceptance by many Christians of the modern age's "pragmatism and secularism" was due largely to the Church's own "fear of new developments." There could be too much respect, he now suggested, for existing institutions. "Before we can properly estimate our place in the world," he noted in *Conjectures,* "we have to get back to the fundamental Christian respect for the *transiency* of both the world and the institutional structures of the Church."

This growing rejection of dogmatic and institutional rigidity, which Merton shared with many contemporary Catholics, was accompanied by an opening out to ecumenism in its broadest sense. As a suitable symbol, Merton revived the mediaeval concept of Christ the Stranger, of the saviour and his angels who might appear at any time, like the begging gods of Greek legend, to test our hospitality; we do not know what guises they may assume. In real life the stranger whom we must welcome as if he were Christ is in fact Everyman, for "every man is, to the Christian, in some sense a brother." Moreover, as Merton remarked in one of his late and posthumously published essays, "Every man at some point in his life encounters God and many who are not Christians have responded to God better than Christians." (*Contemplation in a World of Action*) For the mystical experience that is the gift of God has no respect for the exclusiveness of creeds or doctrines. "There is no reason to think that He cannot impart His light to other men without first consulting us. . . . Nor is there any a priori basis for denying that the great prophetic and religious figures of Islam, Hinduism, Buddhism, etc. could have been mystics in the true, that is, supernatural sense of the word." (*Mystics and Zen Masters*)

Merton called upon Christians to be cautious in adopting the fashions and slogans of the material world at the cost of losing sight of "Christ and His charity," but at the same time he urged them to retain and cultivate the genuine humanism of the Christian cultural tradition in the West, and to broaden their views to include not only all Christian viewpoints but also "all the religious wisdom of the other traditional cultures as well, whether Asian, or primitive American, or African." They should be prepared to collaborate "with all men of good will who are sincerely working for the temporal and spiritual good of the human race." (*Conjectures of a Guilty Bystander*)

During these years Merton enriched his thought and broadened his relationships with men of other faiths both by personal contact and by a pattern of reading that was far more catholic and adventurous than that of his earlier monastic years. In the West, as we shall see in this chapter, he sought out the "separated brethren" of Christianity, the Protestants and those nonbelievers who were so often, as he said of Rimbaud, "Christians turned inside out." The epigraphs to the various sections of *Conjectures of a Guilty Bystander* are themselves fascinating evidence of this broadening of outlook, for their sources include the Chinese poet Po Chu-i, the Moslem mystic Kabir and the English poet Thomas Traherne, Albert Camus, Dietrich Bonhoeffer and Bertolt Brecht, W. H. Auden, St. Thomas Aquinas and Thomas Nashe, while the authors referred to in the journal range widely from Orwell to Nietzsche and from Simone Weil to Julien Green. Merton was opening his vistas with a vengeance!

In one aspect, *Conjectures of a Guilty Bystander* can be regarded as Merton's reconciliation with the Protestantism he left in his young manhood and of which he wrote with such ill-disguised contempt in *The Seven Storey Mountain*. But it is more than an apology for the bad manners of the past. It is a genuine exploration of the insights which Protestants reached on their own during the long centuries of the schism that divided them from the Roman Catholic Church. (And here, though many of them would not agree, we have to include the Anglicans as Merton then saw them: Protestants and non-Catholics in spite of their claim to carry on a genuine apostolic succession.) Merton's approach, as he says in the Preface to the *Conjectures*, which he wrote at the end of 1965, "is completely personal, informal, and tentative. I simply record ways in which theologians like Barth have entered quite naturally and easily into my personal and monastic reflections, indeed, into my own Christian world-view. To put it plainly, the book attempts to show how in actual fact a Catholic monk is able to read Barth and identify with him in much the same way as he would read a Catholic author like Maritain — or indeed a Father of the Church. This is not a critical — if sympathetic — analysis of Protestant thought by a Catholic, but a Catholic sharing the Protestant experience — and other religious experiences as well."

As Merton remarks, he can obviously not be in complete agreement with either Karl Barth or Dietrich Bonhoeffer, who are the most frequently mentioned contemporary Protestant theologians. But he finds their books "relevant and stimulating" in his own peculiar setting of a cloistered contemplative, and he considers that, even from his own special point of view, he profited by approaching them in a spirit of affirmation. "I will be a better Catholic, not if I can *refute* every shade of Protestantism, but if I can affirm the truth in it and still go further. . . . If I affirm myself as a Catholic merely by denying all that is Muslim, Jewish, Protestant, Hindu, Buddhist, etc., in the end I will find that there is not much left for me to affirm as a Catholic; and certainly no breath of the Spirit with which to affirm it."

The three Protestant thinkers to whom he was most attracted were Søren Kierkegaard, Barth, and Bonhoeffer. Kierkegaard, whom despite his Protestantism Merton regarded as "the most sophisticated religious thinker of the last century," had already begun to fascinate Merton even before he entered the Trappist order. There is a significant entry in *The Secular Journal* dated the 29th November, 1940, when Merton was still attracted by the Franciscan order, in which — relating them to "the metaphysics of the 'Dark Night of the Soul'" — he discusses some of the Danish writer's remarks regarding the trial of Abraham when he was commanded to sacrifice Isaac. It is, as Merton remarks, a situation that by any standards of ordinary heroism and by any standards of normal ethics is incomprehensible, since God knows while commanding Abraham to kill Isaac, and Abraham believes when accepting the command, that the murder of his son will not in fact take place.

Kierkegaard may or may not be writing a drama of his own, which may or may not have something to do with the Abraham of the Old Testament. But the important thing is that the terrible and anguishing paradox of the dark night of absolute faith in God is certainly made as clear here as anybody has made it since St. John of the Cross.

All paradoxes are comprehensible, except perhaps the paradoxes that face a few rare souls, who are taken apart by God and confronted not with a test that can be decided in ethical terms, but a test that is according to the ways of God, the ways of eternity, in which nothing is fully comprehensible to us, and nothing is known except terror and silence, and a command. . . .

So, those who have had to suffer, in this way, before God, says Kierkegaard, rising higher than heroes do not become greater than heroes in the eyes of the world, but can only become as nonentities in the eyes of the world, because we cannot understand.

This particular meditation of Kierkegaard was doubtless especially appealing to Merton in 1940, because he was still very much caught up, as he would remain for years afterwards, in the heroic and hence romantic view of the monastic vocation. But there was also the underlying sense—which remained longer with him—of the unpredictability and incomprehensibility of God's grace, which we have to await in fear and trembling and in an uncertainty when only faith—or hope, as Merton later preferred to say—would sustain us. Certainly, in so far as Merton saw the contemplative life in existentialist terms, Kierkegaard was a lasting influence upon him.

But it was Karl Barth, the great Swiss theologian and generator of the modern cult of Kierkegaard, who appealed most to Merton of all the Protestant thinkers. The first pages of *Conjectures of a Guilty Bystander* are dedicated to an affectionate reflection on Karl Barth's devotion to Mozart and his dream of a theological examination which he gave Mozart and in which he tried to draw the musician out by referring to his Masses, but Mozart answered not a word. Barth also remarks that in Mozart's music a child, perhaps "a divine child," speaks to us. And Merton concludes: "Fear not, Karl Barth! Trust in the divine mercy. Though you have grown up to become a theologian, Christ remains a child in you. Your books (and mine) matter less than we might think! There is in us a Mozart who will be our salvation."

Merton developed a remarkable sense of affinity with Barth, whose views on the contemplative life were very close to his own, for Barth also believed that man could only enter into a relationship with God by surrendering his individuality and abandoning himself to the faith that would be granted according to God's will. "The relation of God with this man; the relation of this man with God — this is the only theme of the Bible and of Christianity." Such aphorisms, and such images as Barth's idea of revelation as "the opening of a door that can only be unlocked from the inside," seemed to Merton to express his own thoughts with a boldness he did not always dare to apply to them, and if there was any Protestant he accepted as a true brother, Barth was the man, so that there seemed an extraordinary synchronous appropriateness in the fact that on the same day, the 10th December 1968, Merton died in Bangkok and Barth died in Basel.

Bonhoeffer, like Barth and Merton, was a dedicated ecumenist and a great fighter for human freedom; he was executed in 1945 because of his active opposition to the Nazi tyranny in Germany. Apart from his willingness to sacrifice himself for a just cause, Bonhoeffer appealed to Merton because he supplied what the latter had missed in Barth — an opposition to the kind of dualism that in much Protestant thought separated the Church and the world, the kingdoms of nature and of grace, the sacred and the profane. Bonhoeffer, he said, "emphasizes the rights and dignity of nature in a very Catholic, humanistic way, always in view of 'the ultimate' and the coming of Christ. (What he lacks, from the Catholic viewpoint, is a firm metaphysical basis such as we find in St. Thomas. But his ethic has something of Thomist balance and reasonableness.)" Merton quotes a passage from Bonhoeffer which ends with the sentence: "The life of the body assumes its full significance only with the fulfilment of its inherent claim to joy," and he adds approvingly, "This is a Christian 'worldliness' with which I thoroughly agree." (*Conjectures*)

Merton eventually became so much involved in discussions with American Protestants that a special guest house was built for them in the woods near the Abbey of Gethsemani; when he went into reclusion in 1965 these conferences ceased and the building became his hermitage. He was interested, though by no means in complete agreement, in the proposals for the secularization of Christianity advanced by the Anglican bishop of Woolwich, John A. T. Robinson, in *Honest to God,* and he entered into the famous Death of God controversy which those who claimed to be Bonhoeffer's followers initiated during the 1960s. Merton argued that what seemed to be dying was not really God, but "certain vital possibilities in man himself." "It is the death of spiritual courage which, in spite of all the denials and protestations of commonplace thinking, dares to commit itself irrevocably to belief in a divine principle of life." (*The Monastic Journey*)

Perhaps of all the insights of Protestantism those that Merton admired most related to the problem of saving not the sinner but the "good man." "Those who are faithful to the original grace (I should not say genius) of Protestantism are precisely those who, in all depth, see as Luther saw that the "goodness" of the good may in fact be the greatest religious disaster for a society, and that the crucial problem is the *conversion of the good to Christ.* Kierkegaard sees it, so does Barth, so does Bonhoeffer, so do the Protestant existentialists." (*Conjectures*)

Merton himself was a great castigator of the pharisees, the kind of good men who killed Christ on grounds of principle (he praised Barth's insights into the *unprincipled* nature of much in Christian doctrine), and perhaps there was in this a lingering remnant of his youthful bohemiansim, his dislike of the "squares" (a word he used often in later years), which came alive again in his feeling of affinity during the 1960s with the beats, the hippies and marginal men in general.

Indeed, the picture of his relations with Protestants would not be complete without recording his sympathy with the Shakers, who were certainly a marginal group so far as the "good" Protestant Christians of their time were concerned. With their ecstatic dances, their celibate and cenobitic lives (men and women occupying separate common houses in their villages) and their deeply eschatological cast of mind, the Shakers represented a curious combination of the paramonastic life and the tradition of the mediaeval Cathars or Albigensians, those ecstatic heretics to whom also Merton felt attracted by both compassion and sympathy. He paid several visits to the old Kentucky Shaker colony of Pleasant Hill and was impressed by its lingering peacefulness and by the perfection of Shaker craftsmanship, which to him seemed the outward sign of an inner grace. "The Shakers," he remarked, "have been something of a sign, a mystery, a strange attempt at utter honesty which, in trying perhaps to be too ideally pure, was nevertheless pure — with moments of absurdity." He was interested in the divided attitude of other American Protestants towards the Shakers, whom they hated for their celibate communitarianism and yet whom they unwillingly admired. "Probably they were loved for an angelic gentleness, which after all was related to their celibacy. Thus they were loved for the very thing for which they were hated." (*Conjectures*)

The sign, the mystery, that Merton found in the Shakers he found also in the unbeliever, for he declared that "there *is* a presence of Christ in the unbeliever," and he added — in his own italics — that this presence "*is perhaps the deepest, most cogent mystery of our time.*" He concluded that "The Lord who speaks of freedom in the ground of our being speaks to every man." (*Conjectures*)

This conclusion led Merton to explore not only religious traditions other than the Christian but also the phenomenon, within the world that was still at least culturally Christian, of an anti-religion that in its existential reality, its metaphysical intuitions, might be nearer to true Christianity than many kinds of formal religiosity. God's grace, in other words, obeys no man's logic. In his reading during this period, Merton found himself listening to intriguing and unexpected echoes. He read Orwell and Malraux and rightly found them obsessed with the question of immortality. He found himself responding to uneasy Christians like Charles Péguy and Simone Weil, who preferred to remain on the margin of the Catholic world, "as question marks: questioning not Christ, but Christians."

Existentialism attracted him in its secular almost as much as in its Christian manifestations, and secular existentialism's brother creed, absurdism, interested him so much that — as we shall later see — some of his final poems and imaginative prose works can only be understood if we see them as being at least as firmly within the absurdist anti-tradition as — say — the plays of Ionesco, which Merton greatly admired though he merely read them and never saw them on a stage. He found himself in deep empathy with Albert Camus. "He was one with whom my heart agreed." He found Camus warmer, more human and humbler than Sartre, whom he confesses to having read with excitement and "sometimes with a superficial agreement," though he remarked that Sartre condemned himself to "a puritanism in reverse, a doctrine of justification by sin." Both Sartre and Camus, he claimed, were "inconceivable outside the tradition of Christendom, even though they reject it," and though the dark night of the soul as he conceived it has an ultimate luminosity, he recognized its relationship to the lightless *néant* of Sartre and the other existentialists. "The atheist existentialist has my respect," he remarked; "he accepts his honest despair with stoic dignity. And despair gives his thought a genuine content, because it expresses an experience — a confrontation with emptiness." (*Conjectures*) Even that "blank, godless emptiness" had its echo in the sense of God's absence that was one aspect of the mystical experience, God, at once transcendent and immanent, was at the same time absent and present, and in a mysterious way manifest in emptiness.

The growing attraction that drew Merton towards his opposite and his brother, the unbeliever, cannot be dissociated from his sense — which seemed to be confirmed by the great talk of *aggiornamento* among Catholics at this time — of the temporariness of much of the organizational, ceremonial and even theological aspects of Church life in general and of monasticism in particular. He remarked on how far the new notions of space which science forced upon our minds invalidated "the traditional religious imagery by which we represent to ourselves our encounter with God." The mediaeval cosmology, borrowed from the pagan thinkers of Alexandria, had once seemed a necessary part of the Christian view of the universe, but it had long been discredited and then been found unnecessary, while Christianity remained. Merton recognized that much which passed for ancient practice in the liturgy, whether in the monastery or in secular churches, in fact dated from the sixteenth-century Council of Trent, or from the emergence of Trappism in the seventeenth century, or even from nineteenth-century innovations, and had no precedent either in the primitive Christianity of the first centuries or in the monastic tradition as it was initiated by the Desert Fathers and later by St. Benedict. The same applied to many customs within the monasteries which were regarded as ancient but had in fact been adopted in response to historic circumstances that had long passed away. Thus much of the baggage which the Church had dragged with it into the later twentieth century was antique and dispensable, and if, as some Christian thinkers like Karl Rahner suggested, a diaspora in the sense of a disintegration of traditional organization was inevitable, Merton found himself welcoming the thought. "I am for the diaspora. I prefer it to the closed Medieval hegemony. It may offer better chances of a real Christian life and brotherhood." (*Seeds of Destruction*)

When Merton turned to consider the monasteries, he found them overburdened with usages and forms and practices, including rigid interpretations of obedience, "which have come to stifle the Spirit, though they were useful for keeping monasticism going as an institution." (*Conjectures*) As Merton saw when the flood of postulants ebbed during the 1960s and a reverse flow out of the monasteries began, there was a restiveness in modern young men that rebelled against this restrictive conservatism which a generation earlier, as a young man himself, he had been willing to accept, and he warned his fellow monks against the temptation "to lock the windows and doors in order to keep the Holy Spirit in the monastery."

Considering the present situation of monasticism, Merton attempted to define in basic terms what distinguished the vocation of the monk from other religious vocations. He decided that the minimal definition of monks was that they were "people who have consciously and deliberately adopted a way of life which is marginal with respect to the rest of society, implicitly critical of that society, seeking a certain distance from that society and a freedom from its domination and its imperatives, but nevertheless open to its needs and in dialogue with it." And he went on to describe the monastic life as "in a certain sense scandalous," since "the monk is precisely a man who has no specific task. He is liberated from the routines and servitudes of organized human activity in order to *be free*. Free for what? Free to see, free to praise, free to understand, free to love." (*Contemplation in a World of Action*)

Here we have a view of monasticism which is far different from the conventional idea of monks as men who have adopted slavery to a routine and a ritual in order to escape the responsibilities of life in the world. In part it is a view coloured by Merton's own strong urge to escape from the cenobitic community into the eremitic life in which the kind of freedoms he talked of would more easily be made manifest. But it is also a view not incompatible with that of some of the great monastic founders and reformers, and it is certainly not a view that rejects viable traditions, or dismisses the past and its lessons. It is true that in *Life and Holiness* Merton warned against the kind of self-delusion that manifested itself in a "retreat into a vanished past"; the temporal nostalgia that was so strong in his early self vanished in later years, and though he never became a rampant neophiliac, he was aware of the perils of archaicism.

> The past should live on, and the monk is indeed a preserver of the past. However, the monastery should be something more than a museum. If the monk *merely* keeps in existence monuments of literature and art and thought that would otherwise decay, he is not what he ought to be. He will decay with what is decaying all around him. (*The Monastic Journey*)

It was important, Merton came to realize in his later years, to recognize that the monastic spirit was not necessarily confined to the orders recognized by the Church, nor did it need for its survival organizations of the traditional kind. He found a para-monastic element in many manifestations of the counterculture: in the civil rights and peace movements, in revolutionary groups that had not accepted disciplines imposed by mass political parties, and in the communal ways of living being explored by the beats and the hippies of his time. He envisaged the possibility of "spiritual cells" of clerical or lay contemplatives who would not accept the complete monastic rule, who might include married couples, and who might even combine two vocational paths by being "active contemplatives." Like the regular monks they would be critical of society and as free as possible from its domination while responding to its needs, but their distance from it would not be so great.

The desire to evolve a monastic attitude that would be appropriate to a world in crisis, that would visibly manifest love in that world, led Merton not only to consider with favour the growth of paramonastic communities and movements but also to speak in terms of "a monastic apostolate." In other words, he implicitly recognized that it was not sufficient for the monk to hope that by contemplation alone he could bring about a Christian world or a just and peaceful world of any kind. Obviously there is no point in monks attempting to adopt the vocations that come from "other charisms, foreign to monasticism" such as those of the teaching or nursing or preaching orders. But there is an apostolate that can spring "obviously and manifestly from the monastic life"; an example of such an apostolate would obviously be the shift of Merton's own writing during his last decade towards moral and social criticism. But even here the "freedom" implicit in the monastic way must prevail. "A true monastic apostolate therefore should be 'occasional' in character, and should not be subject to unusual pressures or constant, uninterrupted demands. It should always be an overflow of a deep life of silence and prayer." (*The Monastic Journey*) The monk should approach modern man as a brother and should speak to him not as a superior but an equal. Certainly Merton fulfilled this injunction; in nothing he wrote for a general readership is there any suggestion of talking down from above or of using the special language of an initiate; all is clear, straightforward reasoning.

From such statements one may assume that in Merton's view the monk should try both to create a silent centre for the world and to be a voice speaking to it out of the silence, a Godlike combination of roles. These complementary functions are eloquently expressed in two of those aphoristic sentences in which the poet in Merton gave eloquence to the monk. In 1957, writing of "The Monk in the Changing World," he concluded: "In the night of our technological barbarism, monks must be as trees which exist silently in the dark and by their vital presence purify the air." (*The Monastic Journey*) And in 1968, in the last speech he made, a few hours before his death in Bangkok, he said: "The monk is essentially someone who takes up a critical attitude toward the world and its structures. . . . (*The Asian Journal*)

How this critical attitude demonstrated itself in practice will be seen in the next chapter.

6

The World in a
Grain of Sand

"For my own part," said Merton, "I am by my whole life committed to a certain protest and nonacquiescence, and that is why I am a monk. Yet I know that protest is not enough — is perhaps meaningless." (*Conjectures*) As the years went on Merton found himself impelled more and more to extend his protests beyond the merely silent protest of monasticism: to speak out on issue after issue, and, by implication if not always in direct terms, to sketch out a vision of the just society as he conceived it in earthly form. His solitude became the grain of sand in which he saw the world.

Of course, nobody with an eschatological cast of mind is able to conceive a perfect society except in connection with the Parousia, the coming of Christ and the establishment of his Kingdom and his justice on earth, and for this reason anything a religious thinker like Merton might propose was bound to be provisional, to be bound by the limits that love can attain in this imperfect existence, to be a station on the way to the true Kingdom.

Merton once quoted with approval Berdyaev's remark that once we used to lament that utopias could not be actualized but that now we are faced with the problem of "how to prevent utopias from being actualized." He feared secular utopias because he could not really conceive their being successful without the imposition of a virtually totalitarian degree of authority, and in this he was close to secular men of vision like Orwell and Huxley and Camus. He had once, we have seen, been temporarily a Communist, but even before his entry into Gethsemani he was writing in his *Secular Journal* that people refuse to love their neighbours because they argue that the law or the revolution can take care of social problems, but: "No law will ever abolish poverty. No revolution will ever abolish poverty."

Essentially, the utopian mind is the opposite of the Taoist mind, to whose insights into the autonomy of nature and the natural being Merton was steadily drawing closer, and in the very significant essay, "The Christian in World Crisis," which he wrote around Pope John XXIII's historic encyclical, *Pacem in Terris,* the anti-naturalist and anti-humanist cast of the authoritarian mind, the planning mind, the Machiavellian mind, was exposed. Merton pointed out that:

> ... the totalitarian and absolute concept of authority based on force implies a completely pessimistic view of man and of the world. It is for one reason or another implicitly closed to human values, distrustful or openly contemptuous of reason, fearful of liberty which it cannot distinguish from licence and rebellion. It seeks security in force because it cannot believe that the powers of nature, if left to grow spontaneously, can develop in a sane and healthy fashion. Nature must be controlled with an iron hand because it is evil, or prone to evil; man is perhaps capable of good behavior, but only if he is forced into it by implacable authority. We find this idea cropping up in all kinds of contexts, religious or otherwise, from Calvin to Stalin, from Port Royal to Hitler; there are traces of it in Plato and in St. Augustine; we see it in Fathers of the Church like Tertullian; it provides specious reasons for the Inquisition as well as for Auschwitz. (*Seeds of Destruction*)

Merton believed that the perils of such a concept of authority had been aggravated by the emergence of modern technology, which added another mindless power over man. "If technology remained in the service of what is higher than itself — reason, man, God — it might indeed fulfill some of the functions that are now mythically attributed to it. But becoming autonomous, existing only for itself, it imposes upon man its own irrational demands, and threatens to destroy him. Let us hope it is not too late for man to regain control." (*Conjectures*) One of the disastrous features of the technological revolution was in fact the belief it induced in people that man was now in a position to solve all his problems, given time. "This belief," Merton declared, "is so unfounded that it is itself one of our greatest problems."

Modern technology, unless it were controlled, could only lead, in Merton's view, to a "radical deprivation" in man's "nature and humanity," and the struggle against this and other kinds of alienation might well be the most urgent of the world's needs. On this he rightly tended to agree with Karl Marx, whose theories he had come to reject in many other directions. In the early pages of *Conjectures of a Guilty Bystander* there is a portrait, unusually scathing for Merton and obviously drawn largely from Edmund Wilson's *To the Finland Station,* of Marx's personal failings, the celebrated neuroses that wore a cursing path across his carpet; but then Merton remarks: "Shall we on this account disbelieve everything he said? No, for he was a great diagnostician. He saw the disease of modern man, who has come to be ruled by things and by money, and by machines." And later on, in his essay on "The Christian in World Crisis," Merton elaborates on Marx's insight:

> The subordination of man to the technological process is not something that Marx accepts with unqualified satisfaction. On the contrary it is, for him, the danger and the challenge of a technology based on profit. He thought that the ultimate challenge was for man to free himself from his machines and gain control over them, thus breaking the bonds of alienation and making himself the master of his history.

With all this Merton agreed, except for the idea that man could unaided by God become the master of his history.

Merton was not pessimistic; he shared what he saw as Pope John's essential optimism to the extent of believing that the crisis of our times was an opportunity that we had not yet discovered how to grasp. He saw that crisis and the vast changes it would bring about as unavoidable. Mankind was living in the greatest revolutionary age in history: "a huge, spontaneous upheaval of the entire human race: not the revolution planned and carried out by any particular party, race, or nation, but a deep elemental boiling over of all the inner contradictions that have ever been in man, a revelation of the chaotic forces inside everybody. This is not something we have chosen, nor is it something we are free to avoid." (*Conjectures*) "We must dare to pay the dolorous price of change," he remarked elsewhere, "*to grow into a new society. Nothing else will suffice.*"

Merton was not without hope. He placed great trust, as we shall see, in some of the insurgent forces, such as North America's Negroes. (The term "Black" had not come into acceptance when Merton wrote, and since he always used "Negro" I retain it as historically appropriate.) He found the new radicalism of the counterculture and the early New Left encouraging because—at least in those first years of the 1960s when he was writing—it seemed "far less doctrinaire, less concerned with sweeping political programs, more intent on certain immediate practical ends, especially civil rights and disarmament" than the generation of the 1930s in which he had served his own time as a political rebel. (*Conjectures*) He saw a hope in the role of the monk, whose perspectives of "desert and exile" might give him a special insight into human problems in an age of alienation, and he did not reject the possibility that the unattached individual who exchanged a negative refusal of life for an "intellectual and creative" dissent might find his own ways of escaping from the general confusion of the world. They would presumably be ways analogous to those of the contemplative.

At the same time, while admiring certain radicals, Merton shrank from excess. He saw how self-defeating were most types of activist frenzy. He believed that some of the "extreme progressives" within the Church and even within the religious orders were tending to rely more on Marxism and positivism than on anything that might be "recognizable as Catholic truth." He himself claimed to belong to neither extreme within the Church. "I would like to think I am what Pope John was—a progressive with a deep respect and love for tradition—in other words a progressive who wants to preserve a very clear and marked *continuity* with the past. . . ." (*Conjectures*) Certainly if there was any piece of writing that, apart from the Gospels, provided the basic themes of Merton's Christian radicalism, it was John's *Pacem in Terris,* but Merton had by now become too independent a thinker to play any theme without his own often complex variations.

In his vision of the "new society" Merton was not talking merely of something that would provide a temporary solution to the world's crisis, a merely political solution. He saw it as being embodied in the historic purpose of Christianity, and here he recognized a further resemblance between his thoughts and those of Marx, who was more influenced by the messianic tradition of Judaism than he ever wished to admit.

"We can hope, with Marx," said Merton, "that history has a solution (though we need not believe that history's solution will follow the lines laid down for it by Marx). We can also hope that it is possible for man to guide history towards this hidden solution. Such a belief is not merely compatible with Christianity but essential to it. The Christian religion is eschatological, and the vocation of the individual Christian is to help prepare the final victory of Christ in the world, and the salvation of mankind."

Merton saw the essential problem of creating a new society as one of spiritualizing political principles by a return to the teachings of the Gospel. For him this did not seem an insuperable problem since he believed — with a great deal of historical justification — that even in a secular society, so long as it was democratic and based its freedom on respect for the rights of the human being, the vestiges of spirituality were still there, since "this democratic respect for the person can be traced to the Christian concept that every man is to be regarded as Christ, and treated as Christ." (*Conjectures*)

The great modern problem for the Church, Merton said in *Life and Holiness,* had been "the loss of the working class," but it was in order to establish Christian brotherhood rather than to replenish the ranks of Christians that he called for "Christian social action" in the directions which we nowadays associate with the welfare state — such as better wages, Social Security, etc. — and also in the direction of transforming work itself "so that it becomes for man a source of spiritual renewal, as well as of material livelihood. . . . In a word, if we really understood the meaning of

Christianity in social life we would see it as part of the redemptive work of Christ, liberating man from misery, squalor, subhuman living conditions, economic or political slavery, ignorance, alienation." (*Conjectures*)

This takes us rather far from the monkly life of solitary prayer and praiseful worship, and even in *Life and Holiness,* perhaps the most conventionally devout book Merton wrote during the 1960s, he declared that in a century like ours "it is no longer permissible for Christians to devote themselves seriously and honestly to a spirituality of evasion, a cult of otherworldliness." They must actively manifest their understanding and concern. They must understand that since they are men, their destiny depends on their human behaviour.

Yet Merton realized that there were limits to action in the social and political world so far as monks and priests were concerned. There are occasions in his writings when he looks back with a certain horror on the mediaeval occasions when monks would take up arms and bishops would wield secular power, and he declares emphatically in *Conjectures of a Guilty Bystander* that he does not conceive a Christian society as one run by priests or one that sought to force everyone into regular church attendance. He conceived such a society rather as "one in which work is for production and not for profit, and production is not for its own sake, not merely for the sake of those who own the means of production, but for all who contribute in a constructive way to the process of production. A Christian society is one in which men give their share of labor and intelligence and receive their share of the fruits of the labor of all, and in which all this is seen in relation to a transcendental purpose, the 'history of salvation,' the Kingdom of God, a society centered upon the divine truth and the divine mercy." In such a society the prophetic role of the monk would be fulfilled, in the sense that his renunciation of the right of ownership was an affirmation of God's ownership of everything and of man's right to be a possessor only in so far as he was willing to share with others what he did not need.

From Merton's writings one can assemble some of the features not already mentioned of the kind of society he would have considered good, even though he never set out to create the vision of a detailed Christian utopia. It would be a society made to the human measure, avoiding material or political grandeur in all its aspects and respecting nature through wise environmental policies; Merton did not live to read E. E. Schumacher's *Small is Beautiful,* but if he had, he would have endorsed it. Certainly as far as possible his society would be a de-urbanized one, for: "The metropolis, with all its affluence and all its bursting pride of apparent life, is a center for death." It would be a society purged of the nationalism that sets up the state as the most demanding object of human allegiance. It would be a society in which democracy was interpreted in the sense of a completely free exchangeability of ideas and opinions, no matter how dangerous they may appear. It would be a society created by men who have recognized that "The problem of violence... is not the problem of a few rioters and rebels, but the problem of a whole social structure which is outwardly ordered and respectable, and inwardly ridden by psychopathic obsessions and delusions." It would be a society ruled not by fear but by love of men and also of all living and inanimate things in the created world.

Like many other social visions based on a realistic view of human motives, it seems a rather simple one, like that of the nineteenth-century Christian Socialists and, if one forgets the Christian phraseology, rather like the visions of modest and austere societies based on mutual aid and mutual trust that were imagined by such peaceful anarchists as William Godwin and Peter Kropotkin and Gerrard Winstanley, the seventeenth-century Digger: fellow spirits whom Merton seems never to have encountered on his intellectual pilgrimages.

But visions of simplicity are not always to be realized in simple ways, and Merton was conscious of the deep social problems that must be solved to make such a society possible or even to ensure the survival of the people who might enjoy its benefits, and his writing during the later years — his poetry and more literary work as much as his moral and social criticism — was devoted to what seemed to him the burning questions of the late twentieth century: the question of racism, as demonstrated historically in the persecution of Jews and more immediately in the struggle for a genuine emancipation of the Negro in his own time and country;

the question of war, in the wide sense of the perils of nuclear destruction which had made all past justifications of war obsolete, and in the narrower sense of the war in Vietnam, which for Merton combined the evils of racism and of imperialism with those of sheer inhumanity; the equivocal nature of many human qualities that were once regarded as desirable, such as sanity and obedience, if they were once detached, as they were in the symbolic figure of Adolf Eichmann, from an active moral conscience, a live compassion.

Merton had relatively little direct experience of anti-Semitism. In his childhood and his English youth he moved—as I remember moving in my own English rural childhood at about the same time—in a world from which Jews were virtually absent, so that prejudices about them were never evident. In Germany, in 1932, he was aware—as he tells us in his Preface to *My Argument with the Gestapo*—of the violence within Nazism, but the Nazis were not in power and he did not then witness their anti-Semitism in action; certainly he never at that time foresaw Auschwitz. In New York, at Columbia University, he associated freely with Jews, some of whom became his lifelong friends and one of whom, Robert Lax, followed his example and became a Catholic. After his conversion, Lax visited Merton at Gethsemani, and a curiously sad and symbolic little story about the baptism and its aftermath is told in *The Seven Storey Mountain*:

> They found a Jesuit in that big church up on Park Avenue and he baptized him, and that was that.
> So then Lax had said: "Now I will go to the Trappists in Kentucky and visit Merton."
> Bob Gibney told him: "You were a Jew, and now you are a Catholic. Why don't you black your face? Then you will be all the three things the Southerners hate most."
> The night had already fallen, Christmas Eve, when Lax got to Bardstown. He stood by the road to hitch a ride to the monastery. Some fellows picked him up, and while they were driving along, they began talking about the Jews the way some people talk about the Jews.
> So Lax said that he was not only a Catholic but a converted Jew.

"Oh," said the fellows in the car, "of course, you understand we were talking about *orthodox* Jews."

For Merton, with his passionate devotion to the Psalms and his symbolic and typological interpretation of the Old Testament in general, there was no real division between the Jew and the Christian. The New Testament, he always argued, was the fulfillment of the *spiritual* content of the Old Testament; it was never "a denial of Judaism, but its affirmation." This view he held not merely in his early years at Gethsemani, when he was most influenced by the exaltations of the Psalms, but even in the later period of deep social anxiety when he was searching the Scriptures for the eschatological clues to man's destiny, and when he noted in *Conjectures of a Guilty Bystander* that: "One has either got to be a Jew or stop reading the Bible. The Bible cannot make sense to anyone who is not 'spiritually a Semite.'" Thus his identification with the Jews was based not merely on his empathy with them as a persecuted people, the world's most tragic of marginal men, but also on his vision of Christian tradition emerging out of Judaism and still in spiritual symbiosis with it, and on his eschatological view of human history.

Anti-Semitism, for Merton, appeared under two guises. He saw it among the Nazis as a manifestation of rampant neo-paganism, as an attack not merely on the Jews who became a convenient scapegoat group in a society operated by fear, but even more as "an attack on Christ," a denial, as Karl Barth put it in a passage that Merton approvingly quoted, of the "whole reality of the revelation of God." But he was also perturbed by the more insidious kind of anti-Semitism that exists among Christians who allow their image of the Jews as killers of Christ to hide from them the facts about themselves: that in all their virtue and austerity, in their good-doing and their formal obedience to God and the Church, they are in fact the exact replicas of the Pharisees. "When will we learn" — he sadly asks — "that 'being good' may easily mean having the mentality of a 'Christ-killer'?"

The real point in the story about Robert Lax, so far as Merton is concerned, lies in Gibney's suggestion that Lax should black his face and become — symbolically — a Negro, for the Negroes were the Jews of Merton's life. There was, indeed, no atrocity of Auschwitz or Treblinka that he did not imaginatively undergo, but those worlds of horror still lay outside his experience. The plight of the Negro he witnessed within his own land, and thus it was something he could comprehend existentially, in the time and place where he lived, in the very blood and tissues of the country he had accepted with some emotion as his own when he abandoned his shallow English roots (though not his deeper-running Welsh ancestral heritage) to become an American citizen. And so in the 1960s he came to see the Negro not only as "part of our own sickness" but also as the means by which white men might emerge from that sickness.

For Merton the Negro in America becomes the equivalent of the Jew in Tsarist Russia or Nazi Germany, in that he "is victimized by the psychological and social conflicts now inherent in a white civilization that fears imminent destruction." The problem, essentially, is not merely to extricate the Negro from the role of scapegoat but also to rescue white civilization from the fears and frustrations that make it search for a scapegoat.

Merton's experience of the plight of the Negro went back, as we have seen, to 1940, when Catherine de Hueck Doherty persuaded him to visit Harlem, where he gained an indelible insight into the patience with which at that time the Negroes still endured a deprived and exploited existence. If he had not gone to Gethsemani he would have joined the work in Harlem, and the memory of what he had seen there stayed within him even when he was most single-mindedly endeavouring to turn away from the world into his monastic solitude, so that in *A Man in the Divided Sea,* his second published book of poems which appeared five years after his entry into Gethsemani, he included an aubade entitled "Harlem" and dedicated to Baroness de Hueck; the poignant quatrain that begins and ends the poem is sufficient to show how what he saw there had remained firmly in his mind:

> Across the cages of the keyless aviaries,
> The lines and wires, the gallows of the broken kites,
> Crucify, against the fearful light,
> The ragged dresses of the little children.

It was the courage of the Negro children who marched against police dogs and brutal whip-wielding troopers in Birmingham, Alabama, during the great campaign of civil disobedience led by Martin Luther King in 1963 that most strongly revived Merton's concern over the Negro question. He admired King in the same way he admired Gandhi — as a moral leader who had found a way to incorporate the brotherly dynamic of true Christianity into political action. Merton had inherited his mother's rather vague pacificism, which led him to seek a non-combatant role in case he were drafted in World War II, but it was only with the emergence of the civil rights movement under King's leadership that he began to see with a clear eye the moral and political validity of a non-violent movement aimed at converting the opponent and at benefitting him by releasing him from his sense of guilt — a movement "oriented towards 'healing' the sin of racism and towards unity in reconciliation."

Developing his views of the role of non-violence in the evolution of American society, Merton summarized them in this way: "The purpose of non-violent protest, in its deepest and most spiritual dimensions is then to awaken the conscience of the white man to the awful reality of his injustice and of his sin, so that he will be able to see that the Negro problem is really a *white* problem: that the cancer of injustice and hate which is eating white society and is only partly manifested in racial segregation with all its consequences, *is rooted in the heart of the white man himself.*" (*Seeds of Destruction*) It was in the same way, of course, that Gandhi set out to show that the problems of a subject India were those of the conquerors and not of the conquered.

Merton saw the real difficulties of the American racial situation existing particularly among the white liberals. The southern racist politicians, in his view, showed a kind of brute realism in recognizing the consequences in Negro violence if real equality were not created, and since they had no intention of creating that equality they made their moves accordingly. The white liberals, on the other hand, displayed their unrealism by taking it for granted that the Negro really wanted to become an imitation white man, which of course implied accepting the superiority of the whites. Invited to enter the "lotus-eating commercial society" which the white man had tried to create for himself, the Negro was neither grateful nor impressed; he merely felt that he had been deceived.

Only a society that is radically changed, Merton declares, can bring into actuality the equality of the Negro, and that change can only come about by a recognition—to which he urges his fellow Catholics—that the cultures of the American Negroes and the American whites are different but can be correlated on the basis of equality. With an accurate instinct, Merton recognized the error of the white liberals who worked within the Negro movement and tried to direct it. Under leaders like Martin Luther King, he believed, the Negroes could conduct their own movement with more wisdom than others could do it for them, and he urged white liberals to work within their own society for a reconciliation with the Negroes based on real social justice.

The distance from which he looked out of his monastic reclusion gave Merton a more objective and accurately prophetic view of the situation than many people closer to events acquired as it developed in the United States towards the internal violence of the later 1960s. He saw such violence emerging in revolutionary threats because of the failure of the dominant whites to recognize the realities of a situation that affected their welfare as much as it did that of the suppressed blacks. "Revolutions," he remarked, "are always the result of situations in which the drive of an underprivileged mass of men can no longer be contained by token concessions, and in which the establishment is too confused, too inert and too frightened to *participate* with the underprivileged in a new and creative solution of what is realized to be *their common problem*." (*Seeds of Destruction*)

Merton foresaw the situation becoming more critical as the Negroes realized that civil rights legislation would be evaded and obstructed by the southern whites in order to maintain the old racial dominance. In 1964 he already prophesied the emergence of tougher Negro leaders who would abandon both moderation and non-violent tactics and would mobilize the discontented and unemployed Negroes of the northern city ghettoes in a threat of force. What followed, like the crime already existing in Harlem and similar places, would be the result of the violence done to the

Negro himself by the discrimination that created the ghettoes, by the racist fears that among vast numbers of whites turned into race hatred.

Thinking over the question in *Conjectures of a Guilty Bystander,* Merton concluded: "The Negro is clearly invited to one response. He has had untold reasons for hating the white man. They are now being solidly compounded and confirmed. Even though he has nothing whatever to gain by violence, he has also nothing to lose. And violence will at least be one decisive way of saying what he thinks of white society!"

Up to the early 1960s, as Merton pointed out, there had been — despite the propaganda of the white supremacists — little Communist influence among the Negro militants. But as the situation grew more desperate, he foresaw the infiltration of Maoist influence. At the same time he feared the white backlash, the reaction to Negro violence that might lead to a kind of American fascism that would sweep the well-meaning people up in its course, under the pretext of "running the country" and "keeping order." And in the conclusion to one of his "Letters to a White Liberal," he grimly remarks: ". . . I visualize you, my liberal friend, goose-stepping down Massachusetts Avenue in the uniform of an American Totalitarian Party in a mass rally where nothing but the most uproarious approval is manifest, except, by implication, on the part of silent and strangely scented clouds of smoke drifting over from the new 'camps' where the 'Negroes are living in retirement.'" (*Seeds of Destruction*)

Merton declared that he for one would stand with the Negro, Black Power or no Black Power. "I trust him, I recognize the overwhelming justice of his complaint. I confess I have no right whatever to get in his way, and that as a Christian I owe him my support, not in his ranks but in my own among the whites who refused to trust him or hear him, and who want to destroy him." (*Faith and Violence*) His courage was appreciated by the Negroes — not only by Martin Luther King, who shared his non-violence, but also by the apostle of Black Power, Eldridge Cleaver, who recognized the honesty and insight and love that impelled Merton's statements.

Merton's forebodings were partly justified. The Negroes of

the northern ghettoes in particular regarded the civil rights legislation, which did nothing to improve their economic plight or to relieve their chronic unemployment, as a fraud; many of them turned to violence, but the riots did not turn into revolutions, and the white Americans did not turn to Nazi-like totalitarian politics.

When violence did come to the streets of American cities, it was not motivated only by racist conflict. It sprang also from the deep surge of discontent that produced the new radicalism; for young white Americans that discontent became symbolized in the struggle against the American war of intervention in Vietnam, which itself seemed to represent all that was evil and corrupt and tyrannical in the American political system, all that belied its claims to democracy.

Merton was in total sympathy with those who opposed the war in Vietnam, though, as we shall see, he did not always agree with their methods or their policies. But his concern about war arose before Vietnam became an American public issue, and extended much wider than that particular conflict to the whole question of the immeasurably destructive potentialities of any war in the modern world.

"I will never cease to face the truth which is symbolized in the names Hiroshima, Nagasaki," Merton once wrote to the mayor of Hiroshima, and as the Cold War heated up towards the end of the 1950s he felt impelled to speak out loudly and often against all likely forms of modern war and to reproach the world Catholic community to which he belonged for its failure to take a clear stand on such matters.

Yet there were more apparent inconsistencies in Merton's arguments about war than in most of the other aspects of his social polemics at this period. He was a man of pacifist antecedents. His Quaker mother had persuaded his father, Owen Merton, not to take part in World War I, and he himself in the 1930s had become a pacifist, later registering (after his conversion) for non-combatant service because he did not believe in taking up arms. Yet, although in the 1960s he opposed the one war in which the United States was involved and foresaw that there might be no future armed conflict that he could condone, he was still able to declare: "If a pacifist is one who believes that all war is morally wrong and always has been wrong, then I am not a pacifist."

Here Merton's sense of obedience to the traditions of the post-Augustinian Church tended to shape his words but not his actions. He admitted that early Christian apologists had tended to condemn military service and that Christians like St. Maximilian had been the first men in history to die rather than take up arms against their fellow men. Yet because it had become the tradition of the Church he remained faithful to the idea of the just war that had been accidentally grafted onto Catholic doctrine because of the desperate situation in North Africa during St. Augustine's time, when the Catholic Church was threatened by the Vandal horde that supported the rival Arian bishops.

Merton admitted that even during the middle ages, when it was talked about most ardently, the really just war must have been a rare phenomenon. And he had harsh words for those who believed that such a war might conceivably be waged in the late twentieth century. "Of course when we read Augustine himself, and when we see that he imposes such limits upon the Christian soldier and traces out such a strict line of conduct for him, we can see that the theory of the just war was not altogether absurd, and that it was capable of working in ages less destructive than our own. But one wonders at the modern Augustinians and at their desperate manoeuvres to preserve the doctrine of the just war from the museum or the junk pile." (*Seeds of Destruction*)

In practice, Merton was a pacifist whose defence of the idea of the just war was academic and motivated mostly by a desire to avoid cutting himself off from the mass of his fellow Catholics whom he wished to persuade into opposing nuclear armaments and to whom he suggested the curious compromise position of "relative pacifism." He believed that war in the twentieth century has gone far beyond the point at which morality entered into it. This crucial stage, he pointed out, had been reached even before the atom bomb was first used. During World War II non-combatants were being killed indiscriminately by both sides with ordinary bombing attacks, and in one fire raid on Tokyo as many people were burned to death as died at Hiroshima. "The issue is precisely this; not that atomic and nuclear weapons are immoral while conventional weapons are just, but that *any resort to terrorism and total annihilation* is unjust whatever be the weapons it employs." (*Thomas Merton on Peace*)

Nuclear war, of course, was nothing but war by terror, and it had created a callousness towards human suffering on the part of democratic rulers which one would have found hard to credit in the Nazis before Belsen and Auschwitz went into their relentless cycles of operation. He wrote "and today, while 'experts' calmly discuss the possibility of the United States being able to survive a war if '*only fifty millions*' (!) of the population are killed; when the Chinese speak of being able to *spare* 'Three hundred million' and 'Still get along,' it is obvious that we are no longer in the realm where moral truth is possible." (*Thomas Merton on Peace*) The power of the bomb went beyond its physical effects, and Merton remarked that its use as a weapon of aggression by Christians would mean the spiritual destruction of Christianity itself.

Merton believed that the bomb need not fall, though he certainly did not envisage the balance of fear that — as history has shown us would prevent its being used not only in his life but also for the whole decade after his death. For fear seemed to him an entirely negative force. "The root of all war is fear," he said in *New Seeds of Contemplation:* "not so much the fear men have of one another as the fear they have of *everything*." He saw men striving to negotiate for peace, and failing because their fear overbalanced their genuine good will. We must fearlessly love even the men we cannot trust, he taught; we must not, as so many Catholics did, see Russia or Communism as our real problem, for the enemy was war itself, and peace could not be brought about by hatred: "Peace does not consist in one man, one party, one nation, crushing and dominating everyone else. Peace exists where men who have the power to be enemies are, instead, friends by reason of the sacrifices they have made in order to meet one another on a higher level, where the differences between them are no longer a source of conflict." (*The Monastic Journey*) By such reasoning, Merton brought himself very near to Gandhi's position on war as well as on the struggle for civil rights. He saw non-

violence as not merely the only just means but also the only prac-
ticable one of resisting evil and injustice.

Until Vatican II, in its *Constitution on the Church in the
Modern World,* declared emphatic condemnation of total war,
and hence, by implication, of nuclear war, Merton found himself
at odds with many American Catholics, including a large proportion of the hierarchy, who were either favourable to the idea
of nuclear war—provided it be used against the Communists—
or at least willing to support a defensive nuclear strategy with all
its attendant risks. Merton declared that theologians who did not
publicly condemn all nuclear weaponry as immoral and inhuman
were betraying the traditions of Christian moral teaching, and in
the beginning of 1962 he gave public support to workers who took
part in the January peace strike and called on all Catholics to
refuse any job that contributed to the making of nuclear weapons;
he followed this declaration in February with a Mass dedicated to
anti-war strikers and to peace workers throughout the world.

The Catholic authorities were quickly embarrassed by Merton's one-man campaign, which he carried on in a number of
Catholic and non-Catholic periodicals, and in April 1962, he was
forbidden by his superior to publish any further material on
peace and war. That, he was told, was for bishops and not for
monks to discuss. Merton's response was characteristic. He did
not defy or disobey. Instead, he mailed to sympathizers mimeographed copies of whatever he wrote, and began to consider
means of oral dissemination in case mimeographing were to be
banned. But before that became necessary the whole atmosphere
within the Church had been changed by the effects of Vatican II,
and he was free to resume publication in time to attack a much
more accessible target than nuclear conflict in general: the war
in Vietnam.

Merton saw the Vietnam war as an example in action of
America's peculiar kind of pharisaical nationalism. The Americans, he recognized, tended like the English in the past to see
their country as the centre of the world and therefore to justify
to themselves a business imperialism which involved imposing
their will, always in the name of freedom, on weaker nations

that might stand in their way. When the Vietnamese Buddhist monk and poet, Thich Nhat Hanh, visited the United States to plead for a peace that would be fair to all sides and not just to the people of his country, Merton gave him public support, and declared: "He and I deplore the war that is ravaging his country. We deplore it for exactly the same reasons; human reasons, reasons of sanity, justice and love. We deplore the needless destruction, the fantastic and callous ravaging of human life, the rape of the culture and spirit of an exhausted people." And a little while later, introducing a Vietnamese edition of *No Man Is an Island,* he gave a local habitation to one of Donne's most famous images: "The war in Vietnam is a bell tolling for the whole world, warning the whole world that war may spread everywhere, and violent death may sweep over the entire earth."

Once again, Merton's words made him unpopular with many Catholics, including a number of priests who were chaplains in Vietnam and somewhat bellicose in their role, but this time the Catholic authorities, in the new spirit of Vatican II, did not interfere.

At this period Merton drew as near political activism as he felt his monkly vocation could allow him. In 1962 he sponsored the peace organization called Pax and later the Catholic Peace Fellowship. He contributed articles to liberal and radical Catholic papers like *Commonweal* and the *Catholic Worker,* and he gave moral support to Dorothy Day and other members of the *Catholic Worker* group in the non-violent resistance they organized at the time of the civil defence exercises in New York. He supported the Everyman projects which sent sailing ships manned by pacifists into nuclear test areas in the south Pacific, and he toyed for a while with the idea of participating in the abortive Peace Hostage scheme which would have meant offering himself as a potential victim by going to live in a country which his own might attack.

But he was troubled by the manifest inadequacy of such symbolic protests in the face of the magnitude of the nuclear threat, and in an article written at the beginning of the 1960s he raised pressing questions. "Here we are met with a truly frightening problem. In what does this effective and manifest refusal of consent consist? How does one 'resist'? How are the conscientious objectors to mass suicide going to register their objection and their refusal to co-operate. I do not know." (*Thomas Merton on Peace*)

Other Catholics tried to answer such questions by radical action, and among the handful of priests and members of religious orders who deliberately broke the law and sought imprisonment by dramatic acts of resistance were several to whom Merton was very close in friendship, such as the brothers Daniel and Philip Berrigan. Daniel Berrigan visited Gethsemani in 1962 to address the novices at Merton's invitation, and when he had gone Merton noted appreciatively in his journal:

> Father Dan Berrigan was here: an altogether winning and warm intelligence and a man who, I think, has more than anyone I have ever met the true wide-ranging and simple heart of the Jesuit: zeal, compassion, understanding, and uninhibited religious feeling. Just seeing him restores one's hope in the Church.
>
> The real dimensions of living charity came out clearly in his talks to the novices. They exorcised my weariness, my suspiciousness, my dark thoughts. The community was delighted with him. But I know too that he is not an acceptable man everywhere. (*Conjectures*)

Later, in 1964, the Berrigan brothers and other Catholics, together with some Protestant pacifists like A.J. Muste, took part in a retreat which Merton directed at Gethsemani on the Spiritual Roots of Protest. Five of the participants were later imprisoned for such acts of civil disobedience as raids on draft board offices during 1967 and the destruction of records in such places. In these actions Daniel and Philip Berrigan played leading roles, but how far this was the result of Merton's discourses it is impossible to say.

Merton himself had lamented the lack of active protest among Catholics, but his reaction to the kind of action on which the Berrigans and their associates eventually embarked was ambivalent. He had to be persuaded of the value even of the burning of draft cards by individuals, and he felt that the raids on offices bordered on violence, though he decided in the end that they fitted into the category of true non-violence as distinct from ordinary revolutionary activism because the participants were willing to accept and endure punishment as part of their witness. He showed his moral support for them by dedicating *Faith and Violence,* a collection of his writings on war and peace that appeared in 1968, to Philip Berrigan and James Forest, both of whom were then in prison for their part in the raids and both of whom had attended the retreat at Gethsemani in 1964. But he felt no urge to imitate them. Such activism did not lie within his view of the monastic vocation, and it was not really within his nature to seek it, though there is little doubt that he would have endured any suffering that his own outspoken role as a moral critic might have brought upon him. But he did not regard his protests on paper as in any way heroic, and when he was given the Pax Medal for such writings he was characteristically embarrassed, remarking that he had merely carried out an ordinary Christian duty.

Merton's awakened social concerns were powerfully reflected in his poetry and imaginative essays in the 1960s. He began to experiment with freer forms, he worked in the border areas between poetry and prose, he developed a kind of anti-poetry intended to hold the mind by affronting traditional formal concepts, and just as in his thought he moved closer to the existentialists, so as a writer he found affinities among the absurdists.

He was also ready to explore the work of poets whose ideological positions were far apart from his own. He admired Bertolt Brecht, for example, as a poet rather than a playwright, preferring his work to that of "the esoteric American pontiffs of the day," and remarking that "Brecht is a most individual poet, more so than many who are intensely conscious of their individuality."

He read widely among the Latin American poets, especially the Brazilians, whose Portuguese language he described as "wonderful . . . for poetry" and among whom he found less of the doctrinairism that to him seemed the great fault of so much Latin American poetry. Even the anger of the Marxist poets he did not dismiss; he could hardly do so at a time when anger was entering his own poetry. "Yet this bitterness must be," he said of them; "it is inevitable. I am moved by Alfonso Reyes, and Neruda, both of whom are deeply human, and Neruda remains so in spite of the unutterable banality and pompousness of his party-line exer-

cise books—the later poems." (*Conjectures*) It was the less doctrinaire poets writing in Spanish that he chose to include in the
group of translations concluding *Emblems of a Season of Fury*,
the book of verse he published in 1963. They were Cesar Vallejo
of Peru, Jorge Carrera Andrade of Ecuador, and a trio of Nicara-
guan poets: Ernesto Cardenal, Pablo Antonio Cuadro, and Alfonso Cortes.

Emblems of a Season of Fury is an interesting transitional
book, since it is really a mixture of verse and poetic prose meditations, some of them technological in nature and others emphatically political; the mood varies from the cool serenity of the desert poems about solitude, which continue from an earlier period,
to the concentrated and often deceptively quiet anger of the
poems of moral denunciation.

Outstanding among the poems of the desert in this volume
are "Song: If You Seek . . .," "O Sweet Irrational Worship," and
"Night-flowering Cactus." "Song" embodies the poetic core of
Merton's passion for solitude, which he conceives as the "profes-
sor," the instructor of the seeker after heavenly light. It is solitude
that leads the way into the ultimate emptiness,

> Opening the windows
> Of your innermost apartment.

It is solitude that is "The 'now' that cuts/ Time like a blade,"
that is "the unexpected flash/ Beyond 'yes,' and beyond 'now,'/
The forerunner of the Word of God."

> For I, Solitude, am thine own self:
> I, am Nothingness, am thy All.
> I, Silence, am thy Amen!

"O Sweet Irrational Worship" reflects Merton's joy in the
world of creation. Having read his journals we can imagine him
seated in the grounds of Gethsemani, in the afternoon sun, enjoy-
ing the wind, listening to the call of the little quail called bobwhite. In his meditation the poet's self becomes merged with the
world of creation around him, and he experiences the sweet irrational wonder of God's creatures, who—as he said in another
book—are saints without having, as man does, to will their sanctity.

My heart's love
Bursts with hay and flowers.
I am a lake of blue air
In which my own appointed place
Field and valley
Stand reflected.

I am earth, earth

Out of my grass heart
Rises the bobwhite.

Out of my nameless weeds
His foolish worship.

It is at once near pantheism and far away; there is the pantheistic sense of immersion in the world of nature, but nature — for the pantheist — has no need to worship since it is not God's creation: it is God.

In "Night-flowering Cactus" a new symbol, outside the familiar imagery of mysticism, is found for the ultimate experience of the contemplative: the strange flowering in the darkness that transforms him. In the daytime the cactus appears in the desert in a form resembling the serpent; its night flowering is a "timeless moment of void." It can be descried only dimly, "by divine gift/ As a white cavern without explanation." It speaks with the voice of silence.

When I open once for all my impeccable bell
No one questions my silence:
The all-knowing bird of night flies out of my mouth.

And, like the transcendental experience, it changes all who encounter its inexpressible beauty.

You live for ever in its echo:
You will never be the same again.

The crystal clarity, the formal delicacy of such poems of the desert are qualities that will rarely reappear in Merton's poetry. Indeed, even before *Emblems of a Season of Fury* appeared with these poems from a phase already ended by the time of publication, Merton had issued in 1962 his anti-poem, *Original Child Bomb*. The "original child bomb" was of course that unprece-dented — hence original — monstrosity, the bomb that destroyed Hiroshima. *Original Child Bomb,* which Merton describes in his subtitle as "points for meditation to be scrawled on the walls of a cave," is really a kind of found poem, consisting of slightly ad-apted and condensed snippets from the news reports of the tests at Alamogordo and the bombings of Hiroshima and Nagasaki put together into an ironic narrative whose very baldness and lack of poetic artifice presents the message with stark, quiet di-rectness. For this, like much that Merton would write as poetry from now on, was undisguisedly didactic.

There are poems of this kind in *Emblems of a Season of Fury*. It was nothing new for Merton to introduce social criticism into his verse. Poems in all his earlier books contain this element; outstanding examples are the bitter threnody on urban civili-zation, "In the Ruins of New York," in *Figures for an Apocalypse,* and the morality play, "The Tower of Babel" in *The Strange Islands,* an indictment of materialistic culture based on St. Augustine's teaching that "Two kinds of love have created two Cities: the earthly city is created by the love of self to the point of contempt for God; the heavenly city by love of GOD to the point of self-contempt."

These earlier works, whatever the ideas they embraced, were formally traditional; they were recognizable poems in shape and diction. The anti-poems which form a significant proportion of *Emblems of a Season of Fury* abandon metre and poetic diction and imagery — and even Merton's earlier symbolist assumption that poetry primarily works by suggestion — for the poem as state-ment, even as journalism, reporting in a flat undramatic language facts that are at the same time so banal and so inhuman that they become the images of their own inherent horror. In "A Picture of Lee Ying," Merton meditates on the newspaper photograph of a Chinese girl who has tried to flee to Hong Kong but is being sent back at the border. The officials must obey their orders because the authorities are alarmed, but in consolation the mass media will make sure that she has "the sympathy of millions" and that more will be spent on nuclear weapons. Perhaps in the movies Miss Lee Ying would sail away on a ship after marrying "one of the kind authorities":

> In our movies there is no law higher than love in real
> life duty is higher
>
> You would not want the authorities to neglect duty
>
> How do you like the image of the free world sorry
> you cannot stay
>
> This is the first and last time we will see you in our
> papers.
>
> When you are back home remember us we will be
> having a good time.

The tense understatement of these lines is typical of the poems of protest Merton wrote at this time. Accusations are muted because Merton wishes to show how the enemies of freedom and humanity condemn themselves by their own actions and statements; there is no need for us to denounce them when a diabolical anti-Psalm like "Chant to be used in Processions around a Site with Furnaces" can be constructed by adapting only slightly the self-justificatory statements made by defendants at the trials of those responsible for murdering millions of Jews. And always in these poems there is the echoing suggestion that such crimes are the fault not only of individuals who carry them out but also of the society that allows them and now proposes to sanction different but equal atrocities. As the camp commandant in "Chant" ends his statement:

> You smile at my career but you would do as I did if you knew
> yourself and dared
>
> In my day we worked hard we saw what we did our
> self-sacrifice was conscientious and complete our work
> was faultless and detailed
>
> Do not think yourself better because you burn up
> friends and enemies with long-range missiles without
> ever seeing what you have done

How can we, as sane and conscientious people, be thought capable of such acts? Perhaps our very sanity, our very conscientiousness detached from spiritual insight, may be the factors that make us so capable. This is the question Merton discusses tellingly in the volume of essays and fantasies, *Raids on the Unspeakable,* which appeared in 1966. *Raids* is a mixture of formal essays and meditations on literature and life, and its contents suggest — if one compares them with a volume of essays by some omnivorous reader-critic like Edmund Wilson or George Orwell — that if Merton was a man of letters he was not in the broader sense a literary man. He did not really read for the joy of reading or for the sake of literature as an art, and so the writers and subjects he discusses tend to be limited by his philosophic interests and by the luck of his desultory reading rather than by a deep interest in the literary culture for its own sake. How else can one explain a collection in which the writers picked out for discussion are such a strange trio as Ionesco, Julien Green and Flannery O'Connor?

Perhaps the choice of Ionesco is the most significant. He appears in an essay-meditation entitled "Rain and the Rhinoceros." Here, musing Thoreau-like in his remote hermitage, Merton considers the people of the cities who "have constructed a world outside the world, against the world, a world of mechanical fictions which contemn nature and seek only to use it up, thus preventing it from renewing itself and man." Isolated from nature, isolated from the loneliness in which the solitary, "far from enclosing himself, becomes every man," the world of unrenewed urban humanity develops, in Merton's view, into the world of Ionesco's *Rhinoceros.* In that play, having lost the sense of what it means to be human, human beings turn into rhinoceroses, with a consequent inversion of values by which the last man in a rhinoceros herd himself becomes a monstrosity. Merton goes on to quote with approval Ionesco's statements relating to his play which, as he says, bring the playwright "very close to Zen and to Christian eremitism," for Ionesco declares that "The universal and modern man is the man in a rush (i.e. a rhinoceros), a man who has no time, who is a prisoner of necessity....," one of those who "have lost the sense and the taste for solitude." And

Merton, meditating in his rainy woods, shares Ionesco's feeling that "there will always be a place for those isolated consciences who have stood up for the universal conscience as against the mass mind." At the same time he cannot deafen himself to the fact that, while the quail are whistling in the wet bushes, "even here the earth shakes. Over at Fort Knox the Rhinoceros is having fun."

Ionesco's absurdism tempted Merton into a formal experimentation as well as a kind of existentialist world view, and one of the most impressive items in *Raids on the Unspeakable* is a prose fantasy entitled "Atlas and the Fatman," in which Merton seeks to develop his concept of the Unspeakable. The Unspeakable is really the anti-void, the emptiness that is never filled, the end that does not mean a beginning, the reign — though Merton does not use the term — of the antiChrist whose realm mediaeval men believed must precede the Parousia. As he does put it, it is "Not necessarily the end of the world, but a theological point of no return, a climax of absolute finality in refusal, in equivocation, in disorder, in absurdity, which can be broken open again to truth only by miracle, by the coming of God." And the Unspeakable — the Fatman of the story — can be interpreted, according to one's wish, as Hitler or Stalin or antiChrist, but the disturbing feature of Merton's fantasy lies in the fact that Fatman is really the product of our own nightmares and could be shrugged off as easily as Atlas (that sentient mountain who represents "the world *as good*") finally shrugs him off, if only we learned not to fear.

Raids on the Unspeakable includes a variety of other valuable essays, including some astute comments on the role of the poet and the artist and their relations with the political life of their time (one cannot avoid it but must not drown in it, would fairly summarize Merton's view), but undoubtedly the most disquieting and the most important for its centrality to the concerns of Merton's later years is "A Devout Meditation on Adolf Eichmann." The Eichmann case fascinated Merton, and even before he wrote the "Devout Meditation" he had noted in the journal that became *Conjectures of a Guilty Bystander:*

The Eichmann story shows the breakdown of forensic concepts of morality and demands an existential respect for the human reality of each situation. Without this respect, principles will never regain their meaning in concrete life. Meanwhile, there is no legal machinery to deal with such moral disasters. What judgment could *add anything* to the judgment already implied in the fact that a man who was by certain accepted standards quite honest, respectable, sane, and efficient could do the things he did without feeling that he was wrong? This judgment falls not on Eichmann alone, but on our whole society. What then is the significance of a special judgment pronounced upon Eichmann by our society? This is the real question.

It was the last thought he developed in the "Devout Meditation." Of Eichmann's sanity, of his conventional honesty, of his loyalty and incorruptibility in the accepted sense there could be no doubt; the appalling reality was that these very qualities, divorced from other qualities, had fitted Eichmann for his grim tasks. But this fact cuts the ground from under some of our cherished conceptions of the ideal leaders of men. "The sanity of Eichmann is disturbing. We equate sanity with a sense of justice, with humaneness, with prudence, with the capacity to love and understand other people. We rely on the sane people of the world to preserve it from barbarism, madness, destruction. And now it begins to dawn on us that it is precisely the *sane* ones who are the most dangerous."

Merton does not waste his time dwelling on Eichmann personally. He is concerned with future Eichmanns, men of sanity and efficiency who will be in key positions during the great crises of the nuclear age. It is not the madmen we must fear; they will never be allowed into the positions that govern matters of universal life and death. "The sane ones will keep them far from the button. No one suspects the sane, and the sane ones will have *perfectly good reasons,* logical, well-adjusted reasons, for firing the shot. They will be obeying sane orders that have come sanely down the chain of command. And because of their sanity they will have no qualms at all. When the missiles take off, then, *it will be no mistake.*"

Merton asks himself what is the meaning or value of a concept of sanity that considers love irrelevant, and he reaches the conclusion that sanity as men in the West view it is of no more use than "the huge bulk and muscles of the dinosaur." The possibility of survival, he suggests, lies in less rather than more sanity, in a diminished self-assurance, in a greater consciousness of human absurdities and contradictions. "Perhaps we must say that in a society like ours, the worst insanity is to be totally without anxiety, totally 'sane.'"

To abdicate the belief in total sanity is to acknowledge the world as absurd. From absurdism to Taoism and Zen and Sufism is not a long road, and Merton took it.

7

The Call of Asia

"One of the most significant facts about the life and vocation of Gandhi," Thomas Merton once said, "was his discovery of the East through the West." Gandhi, who had left India with the idea of becoming an imitation Englishman like many of his alienated fellow countrymen, discovered his own tradition in the West when he first read the *Bhagavad Gita* in an English translation. This awakening to his own culture in a distant land did not make Gandhi forget what the West had taught him; the Bible and Tolstoy, Ruskin and Thoreau, continued to nourish him mentally and spiritually, just as the writings of the Moslems and Hindus did in India, so that he became at once a traditional Hindu teacher leading his people towards freedom and — less successfully — towards the realization of their true selves, and also one of the most broadly ecumenical men the world has ever known, combining Christianity and Buddhism and Islam with his own traditional Hinduism both in the simple ceremonial of the paramonastic ashrams that grew up around him and in his political thought and practice.

Merton's inner development — if not his external career — was in some ways remarkably similar to Gandhi's, except that the direction was reversed and Merton came to his discovery of the West through the East. As a schoolboy in England he was already fascinated by Gandhi's struggle in the guise of a minute David against the Goliath of British imperialism, and took up his defence when conservative schoolfellows attacked the Indian leader. Later, at Columbia, in the days of mental searching after Communism had failed to satisfy him, he encountered an Indian holy man named Bramachari who had found his way to the United States long before such figures became fashionable and financially successful in the West. Merton had read Aldous Huxley's references in *Ends and Means* to Asian mysticism and had come away with "the prejudice that Christianity was a less pure religion"; he had ransacked the university library for books on Asian mysticism and spent hours reading "the Jesuit Father Weiger's French translation of hundreds of strange Oriental texts," from which at the time he learned almost nothing, coming away with little more than an impression of the "Absolute Being" as "an infinite, timeless, peaceful Nothing."

It was then that Bramachari, whom he asked for advice, said to him ("not without a certain earnestness"): "There are many beautiful mystical books written by the Christians. You should read *St. Augustine's Confessions* and *The Imitation of Christ.*" Reading these books, on the insistent recommendation of an Indian *sanyasin* marooned in New York, turned Merton back into the road that led him to his conversion to Catholicism and to the realization of his monastic vocation. Later, when he reflected on these circumstances, Merton felt it to be "very probable that one of the reasons why God had brought him all the way from India, was that he might say just that." It was a pardonable lapse into self-complacency.

If Gandhi retained to good purpose his interest in the western literature of religiously oriented activism, Merton did not lose interest in Asian writings on mysticism. In the end he wrote no less than five books reflecting that interest: *Gandhi on Non-Violence* (1965), *The Way of Chuang Tzu* (1965), *Mystics and Zen Masters* (1967), *Zen and the Birds of Appetite* (1968), and the posthumously published *Asian Journal* (1973). One should not be misled by the dates of these books into assuming that they represent an interest that revived in the last four or five years of Merton's life. Some of them are collections of essays of which the earliest appeared in 1961, and Merton tells us that *The Way of Chuang Tzu* represented "Five years of reading, study, annotation and meditation," so that the preparation for it went at least as far back as 1960. Moreover, there is the extraordinary "General Dance" chapter which ends *New Seeds of Contemplation*; a chapter completed, to judge from the date of the ecclesiastical imprimatur, early in 1961. Not only does this rhapsodic evocation of God's "mysterious cosmic dance" bring to mind the Hindu concept of the cosmic dance of Siva but also there is a specific reference to the Japanese poet Basho hearing "an old frog land in a quiet pool with a solitary splash" which is clearly a clue intended to tell us firstly that Merton had been reading Zen poets and more importantly that he believed it was not given to Christians alone to catch "a glimpse of the cosmic dance."

And there are other clues which suggest that even when Merton was most immersed in the monastic life and in the exhausting experience of becoming a priest, the interest in Asian religions and especially in Asian contemplative ways was reviving. *The Sign of Jonas*, for example, contains an entry dated the 24th November, 1949, in which Merton talks of corresponding with an Indian in Simla about Patanjali's yoga and mentions a chemist visiting the monastery who had been a postulant in a Zen Buddhist monastery in Hawaii and had talked to the monks at Gethsemani about his experiences.

Merton's approach to Asian religions was not a simple one. He believed, to begin, that if mankind were to be made whole again, if the world were to be healed of the spiritual disorders that led to material disasters, there must be a rapprochement between the East and the West, and especially between the adherents of eastern and western religions, and that as part of the process the Church should open itself to learning from the eastern religions as in its early days it had been exposed to the philosophic influences of Platonism and Gnosticism and in the middle ages to the teachings of Aristotle and the Arab Islamic theologians.

But, as a practising contemplative, Merton was also interested in the similarities between Asian and European mystical traditions. And, finally, he seems to have felt a strong personal affinity towards the Asians and their ways of thinking. He recorded that when he met the great Zen scholar Daisetz Suzuki he decided they were "fellow citizens," and in the Preface to the translation of *The Seven Storey Mountain* he recorded that he felt himself "much closer to the Zen monks of ancient Japan than to the busy and impatient men of the west."

In an essay on pilgrimages and crusades included in *Mystics and Zen Masters,* Merton talks of the wandering inclinations of the Celtic monks of the early middle ages. "The geographical pilgrimage," he remarked, "is the symbolic acting out of an inner journey." And one could very well apply this insight to Merton's own life. The journey on which he died was indeed a pilgrimage, to the surviving sources of Asian religious wisdom, but it was also the culmination of an inner journey he had started long before, when he began mentally to explore the frontiers of the Christian world, up to and finally beyond the remotenesses where the early eremitic fathers meditated. Alexandria, that great cosmopolis so near to the desert, always fascinated him and in the years before his death he thought often of devoting time to a thorough study of that intellectual rendezvous of the ancient world where Christianity encountered the philosophies of classical antiquity and the Asian cults that Hellenistic imperialism had gathered in to this glittering centre.

But there was not time for such a work, and Merton's interests leapt beyond Alexandria, even beyond the Moslem world, though as a religion of the wilderness Islam interested him, and he wrote of the *Koran:*"It moves me deeply, with its spirit of loneliness, independence of men, dependence on God, emptiness, trust — the spirit of the desert which, for Muslims, is not the prerogative of a few." (*Conjectures*) It is true that Merton was familiar with Sufism, and the Sufis are always there as background presences in his writings, but it was Zen and Taoism in China and Japan as contemplative movements, and Gandhi in India as a personality, that most attracted his attention.

Gandhi he saw as the man who had developed a means by which the gifts of the contemplative life could be brought to bear on the life of men in society. Gandhi set out to demonstrate that there is a *"universally valid* spiritual tradition which he saw to be common to both East and West" and also that the "spiritual or interior life is not an exclusively private affair." In a career that was eminently active, he maintained intact the contemplative element, and this emerged in his *satyagraha,* the non-violence which he significantly called "truth force," and which, as Merton points out, must be understood not as a means to achieving unity but as "the fruit of inner unity already achieved." With admirable conciseness and clarity Merton summarizes Gandhi's essential concept:

> This is his lesson and his legacy to the world: The evils we suffer cannot be eliminated by a violent attack in which one sector of humanity flies at another in destructive fury. Our evils are common and the solution of them can only be common. But we are not ready to undertake this common task because we are not ourselves. Consequently the first duty of every man is to return to his own "right mind" in order that society itself may be sane. (*Gandhi on Non-Violence*)

Gandhi, in fact, applied the principles of the Gospel to political and social problems through an approach that was "inseparably religious and political at the same time," and this was what made him unique among the world leaders of our age.

> It is certainly true that Gandhi was not above all criticism; no man is. But it is evident that he was unlike all the other world leaders of his time in that his life was marked by a wholeness and a wisdom, an integrity and a spiritual consistency that the others lacked, or manifested only in reverse, in consistent fidelity to a dynamism of evil and destruction. . . . His way was no secret: it was simply to follow conscience without regard for the consequences to himself, in the belief that this was demanded of him by God and that the results would be the work of God. (*Seeds of Destruction*)

It is interesting to observe how near Merton comes in his estimate of Gandhi to that very different observer, George Orwell, who specifically rejected any claims that might be made for Gandhi's sainthood, and yet concluded, "regarded simply as a politician, and compared with the other leading political figures of our time, how clean a smell he has managed to leave behind."

Gandhi inspired Merton's admiration by the integrity that enabled him to dissociate himself from evil with total disregard for the consequences. He filled him with a degree of wonder as one of the great martyr-saints of our age. Yet the real reason why Merton spent time compiling *Gandhi on Non-Violence* was that he believed the Gandhian teachings on civil disobedience were of urgent importance to the world and especially to the America of the 1960s. Here, in a little over fifty pages of extracts, he was able to present the principles and the rules of conduct which those who fought for peace and civil rights should follow. Ideally, Merton believed, America also should follow them in its relations with other countries.

They were the rules Gandhi had developed existentially, in the practice and suffering of his long struggles for justice in South Africa and for freedom in India, and they had worked. "Gandhi," as Merton said in his introductory essay on "Gandhi and the One-Eyed Giant," "was dedicated to peace, and though he was engaged in a bitter struggle for national liberation, he achieved this by peaceful means. He believed in serving the truth by non-violence, and his non-violence was effective in so far as it began first within himself." Gandhi did not attempt to evade or deny the presence of evil when he encountered it; instead, through non-violence proceeding from an inner liberation, he learned how "to use the force and the presence of evil as a fulcrum for good and for liberation." It was Gandhi's non-violence that Merton, like Martin Luther King, supported as the basic strategy of the Negro's struggle for liberation, and it was non-violence that he opposed to revolution (by which he meant violent revolution) as a means of social change. Gandhi, for whom "the public realm was not secular, it was sacred," seemed to have realized the hope Merton had acquired from Aldous Huxley long ago—that the presence of spiritually awakened men can change society in ways no ordinary political methods can imitate.

In the end Gandhi failed politically; he knew it, and Merton admits it. The India that emerged into freedom in 1947 had not found itself in truth as Gandhi hoped; in shedding the imperial yoke, it split into two mutually hostile nation-states dependent on violence like any other militaristic society. But once we go beyond immediate political effects, it is difficult to tell what influence the truth may eventually have; one cannot judge such matters with easy pragmatism. The truth, once uttered, is not dead; it can—as Gandhi believed—be recovered, and the Gandhian truth which Merton hoped might be recovered in his own time taught that "there can be no peace on earth without the kind of inner change that brings man back to his 'right mind.'" That kind of change, though Merton does not say so explicitly, is the self-transcendence at which contemplatives in all religions aim.

It was to the furthering of mutual understanding among such contemplatives, as a preparation for wider understandings between East and West, that Merton devoted much energy in his last years, and in its service he went on the journey that ended in his death. His concern for such understanding was linked necessarily with his anxiety over the destructive forces that seemed to be so active in the world of his time. "If the West continues to underestimate and to neglect the spiritual heritage of the East, it may hasten the tragedy that threatens man and his civilizations," he argued in *Mystics and Zen Masters*. ". . . The horizons of the world are no longer confined to Europe and America. We have to gain new perspectives, and on this our spiritual and even our physical survival may depend."

The history of the early seventeenth-century Jesuit missionaries to China was for Merton a salutory example both of right conduct on the part of Catholics and of tragic misunderstanding within the Catholic Church. When they reached China, with their maps and their clocks and their astronomical instruments, the Jesuits realized that they were entering a high civilization with its own way of objectifying spiritual experiences. They perceived the good in Chinese Buddhism, in Taoism and Confucianism. They studied these native traditions with such application and understanding that they became scholars of recognized standing within the exclusive mandarin community, whose costumes and customs they adopted. As Merton said of Matthew Ricci: "Like a true missionary, he divested himself of all that belonged to his own country and his own race and adopted all the good customs and attitudes of the land to which he had been sent."

The Jesuit missionaries were accepted in China both for their great learning and for the respect they showed for Chinese culture: they recognized that cultural differences had no real bearing on the essential truths of religion. Hence, having understood that the Confucian ceremonies expressing respect for the ancestors were in no way idolatrous, they allowed their converts to follow these "Chinese rites," and they proposed to Rome — centuries ahead of the reforms that followed Vatican II — the creation of a vernacular liturgy for the Chinese, who found Latin extremely hard to follow and even more difficult to speak. Unfortunately the Jesuit fathers undertook their pioneer mission to China during the Church's period of defensive orthodoxy following the Council of Trent. Other missionary orders, more inclined to the sixteenth-century methods of conversion by the sword which had destroyed the native high cultures of the Americas, used their influence jealously to prevent the acceptance by the Vatican of the Jesuit methods, and the work done by Ricci and his companions was destroyed by the withdrawal of papal support. A splendid opportunity for fostering understanding between the East and the West had been lost, and it would not be offered again as antagonism built up between the Chinese and the red-haired foreign devils, as they were soon to describe the European intruders.

Yet Merton believed that, in this "brief epiphany of the Son of Man as a Chinese scholar," the seventeenth-century Jesuits had set an example to modern Catholics of the kind of dialogue that must be established with the world's non-Christian religions, and in his own time he was impressed by the fact that it was Jesuits in the 1960s who had found the courage and curiosity to learn about Zen by practising it in Japanese Zen monasteries.

Merton would have been the last man to gloss over the theological differences between Christianity and the religions of Asia. For him, only Christianity looked to what in *Mystics and Zen Masters* he called "the transcendent and personal center" which is "the Risen and Deathless Christ in Whom all are fulfilled in One." Yet, as he suggested abundantly in his writings on Taoism and on various forms of Buddhism, there were tantalizing approaches within these Asian mystical traditions to what one normally regards as exclusively Christian beliefs and practices, and below this level of perhaps deceptive superficial resemblances there were levels at which, freed from the divisive factors of liturgy and dogma, men of many faiths could meet and share their spiritual insights.

> The great contemplative traditions of East and West, while differing sometimes quite radically in their formulation of their aims and in their understanding of their methods, agree in thinking that by spiritual disciplines a man can radically change his life and attain to a deeper meaning, a more perfect integration, a more complete fulfillment, a more total liberty of spirit than are possible routines of a purely active existence centered on money-making. (*Mystics and Zen Masters*)

It was in this spirit that Merton himself, when in the last months of his life he became a wanderer rather than an eremite, set out his great Asian journey. "I come as a pilgrim," he said, "who is anxious to obtain not just information, not just 'facts' about other monastic traditions, but to drink from ancient sources of monastic vision and experience. I seek not only to learn more (quantitatively) about religion and about monastic life, but to become a better and more enlightened monk (qualitatively) myself." (*The Asian Journal*)

Merton hoped these things for himself, but also, perhaps naively, given the eager Asian acceptance in the mid-century of western values as well as western technologies, he hoped for modern man in general a "liberation from his inordinate self-consciousness, his monumental self-awareness, his obsession with self-affirmation, so that he may enjoy the freedom from concern that goes with being simply what he is and accepting things as they are in order to work with them as he can."

Here, it must be emphasized, Merton was not a typical Catholic — not even a typical Catholic of the post-Vatican II era. As he pointed out, both the conservatives and the progressives within the Church were suspicious of Asian religions. "Conservatives because they think all Asian religious thought is pantheistic and incompatible with the Christian belief in God as Creator. Progressives because they think all Asian religions are purely and simply world-denying evasions into trance. . . ." This resulted in the curious situation of the contemplatives being ahead of the rest of

Christianity, for "only the Catholics who are still convinced of the importance of Christian mysticism are also aware that much is to be learned from a study of the techniques and experience of Oriental religions." (*Zen and the Birds of Appetite*)

Having travelled during the 1960s and 1970s a good deal more extensively than Merton in Asia and Oceania, in Latin America and the Canadian Arctic and other areas where Christian missionaries are still active, I am impelled to say that Merton is somewhat unjust to other kinds of Christians, and especially to Catholics who do not sustain his own passionate interest in mysticism. Except for a few groups of evangelical fundamentalists who operate largely by raiding the flocks of other Christian sects, missionaries—especially when they work among non-Christians—are nowadays much less eager to make converts than to establish a brotherly dialogue in which the basic element of justice or charity or love, or whatever else the individual may choose to call it, is exemplified in an attempt to rectify inequalities between peoples whose creeds may differ but whose basic religious intuitions may be remarkably similar. Having said so much, one may accept Merton's contention that such a rapprochement is facilitated by the recognition that Christian mysticism and Asian non-theistic mysticism "really seek to express the same kind of consciousness or at least to approach it in varying ways."

Merton himself was attracted—among Asian religious traditions—principally to Taoism and Zen, and afterwards to Tibetan Mahayanist Buddhism. He was less closely interested in the varieties of Hinduism and in the Theravada Buddhism of Ceylon, Burma and Thailand. It is tempting to suggest that the neglect of Theravada Buddhism was due to the fact that the rival Mahayanist Buddhism finds room for the saviour figure in the form of the Bodhisattva who postpones his own Nirvana until all living beings have attained enlightenment. But in fact Merton showed little interest in this aspect of the Mahayanist tradition, which in the Pure Land Buddhism of Japan develops into a veritable salvationist movement. Zen, which interested him most, is in fact the strain of Mahayanist Buddhism least influenced by the Bodhisattvic tradition, and classical Taoism, with its rooted horror for any kind of good-doing that may restrict the true flowering of man's nature in the way of Tao, was openly and contemptuously anti-salvationist.

The Taoism of China's classical age was, as Merton repeatedly emphasized, a great deal different from the degenerate mixture of superstition and nature cultism, of magic and alchemy and soothsaying, that in recent centuries has passed under the same name. Taoism was indeed always a way, with an emphasis on the organic nature of a way as distinct from a formally organized religion, that based itself on man's archetypal perceptions of the cosmos, an ancient culture of the kind "that enabled man to live according to the light of wisdom immanent in the world and in the society of which he formed a part." (*Conjectures*) The difference between the Taoism of the fourth century BC, which fascinated Merton, and recent Taoism is perhaps mainly due to the fact that early Taoism was nearer to the pristine reflections on their relationship with nature of men in a neolithic age before humanity became involved in the complexities of urban living.

Why should Merton have been so attracted to early Taoism, and especially to a Taoist thinker and poet like Chuang Tzu, who lived more than three centuries before Christ? I think the attractions were very similar to those that drew him towards the Christian Desert Fathers. There was a nostalgic yearning back to simpler ages in the world's history, ages that took on a certain mythical quality because they were nearer in spirit to the earthly paradise which in fact they sought to recreate, as Merton in his turn sought to recreate the modified paradise of the eremitic life; ages in which, whatever the dominant religious tradition, "every aspect of life was seen in relation to the sacred."

There is also the attraction of a unique personality that still, after more than two millennia, emerges with remarkable vividness and warmth out of Chuang Tzu's discourses, and this despite all his Taoist preaching that the wise man must assume a profile low almost to the point of invisibility. Chuang Tzu evidently enjoys with total acceptance a world he has no desire to control or possess, a world where all beings should live without interference according to their natures:

Water is for fish
And air for men.
Natures differ, and needs with them.

Hence the wise men of old
Did not lay down
One measure for all.

It was a way of perception extremely agreeable to the Merton who
gloried in the splendour of God's creation.

Power, Chuang Tzu despises as much as wealth; he looks
with a quietly compassionate amusement on the strivings of men,
but he does not castigate them in the manner of a denunciatory
prophet; irony and the mocking parable are his tools. Using them
skillfully, he creates a sharply imaged, concrete and concisely
aphoristic way of writing, which, like his master Lao Tzu's *Tao
Te Ching,* and like the Psalms in a somewhat different way, is
nearer to poetry than it is to preaching. That Merton appreciated
the poet in Chuang Tzu is shown by the skill and lyrical appeal
of his English versions, which he prepared with the help of various
translations and of John Wu, a Chinese Catholic scholar. Merton
began to study Chinese, but he never learned enough for translation, and this may have been as well, since what he did produce
by the rather complex method he followed were versions that
are accurate enough not to have been challenged, and which
stand as English poems in their own right, like Waley's and Pound's
translations.

Apart from a poet's interest in another poet-contemplative
and in an archaic age, it is the solitary contemplative in Merton,
I believe, who was attracted to Chuang Tzu and to Taoism in
general, while the cenobitic contemplative was attracted to Zen.
The side of his mind that was drawn to Thoreau was drawn also
to Tao.

What made Chuang Tzu's writings and the supposed sayings
of Lao Tzu appealing to many Europeans when popular translations began to appear in the later nineteenth century was their
apolitical nature and their apparently libertarian inclinations.
Peter Kropotkin accepted Lao Tzu — who said that "To organize
is to destroy" — into the pantheon of anarchism; Oscar Wilde

hailed with the delight of a fellow aphorist what he regarded as the purely aestheticist implications of such dicta of Chuang Tzu as: "Every man knows how useful it is to be useful./ No one seems to know/ How useful it is to be useless."

I think there was an infrequently expressed facet of Merton's mind (the suppressed facet which once made him say that if he had not believed in God, conscience would have made him an anarchist) that found this aspect of Chuang Tzu and the Taoists very appealing, particularly at a time when his fear of power in the hands of sane as well as insane men made him appreciate Chuang Tzu's acerbic remarks about those who were controlled by the ambition to wield authority.

But most of all, it was the whole concept of the Tao and man's relationship to it that interested Merton for its analogical resemblances to some of the insights of Christian contemplatives. The idea of the understanding that is "Tao's gift" but cannot be striven for is superficially similar to God's gift of grace, and parallel to the concept of the dark night of the soul is the sense of Tao being apprehended only when the intellectual process has ceased to work, "where there is no longer word or silence."

Yet at the same time very little of the familiar imagery of Christian mysticism appears in Chuang Tzu, and I believe that this absence represents more than a difference of cultures, and that Taoism is not in the accepted sense a mystical doctrine; it is not basically concerned with the same kind of experiences as those which St. John of the Cross or Meister Eckhart described. It is in a very literal sense a way, a mode of living that recognizes the existence of universal forces — something close to what we call natural laws — and which holds that man can live according to these forces, and can benefit from them, by ceasing to be conscious of any distinction between himself and the world around him. He must indeed, like the Christian mystic, empty himself, but what then works through him is not in any sense a transcendental Spirit; it is Tao, which comprehends all contradictions, which "assembles and destroys," which is neither the Totality nor the Void, which is and is not, which "acts and has no form." The rule of living under Tao is simple — *wu-wei,* doing nothing. But it is not the way of quietism nor is *wu-wei* really inaction. The wise man disregards the Self and thus acquires emptiness, from which comes stillness; it is out of stillness, by flowing as it were with the currents of nature, that action emerges and attainment emerges from action.

It is easy to see the attractive resemblances between aspects of such a teaching and Merton's own view of the Christian contemplative way as distinct from that way's destination, if one can indeed make such a distinction between means and ends. There is the sense of the power that "acts and has no form"; there is the sense of emptying oneself for that power to flow into one; there is the sense that out of inner stillness can come the kind of action and attainment that are not evil. Yet the fact remains that the Taoist is not seeking a mystical union with a God that is transcendental as well as immanent; that there is no question of a false ego being dissolved to liberate a true Self, an inner man, since any kind of Self to the Taoist is an impediment to man's apprehending the true "nature" by which he takes his place in the universe; there is no sense of the need for self-transcendence among Taoists as it appears among Christians and among certain Mahayanist Buddhists, since the very idea of transcendence is alien to a belief that in Tao all beings must live according to their natures; there is no ecstatic experience that lifts the Taoist out of humanity, that divinizes or at least sanctifies him as true mystical experiences in Christianity are held to do.

The essential immanentism of Taoism, its obvious links with preliterate and probably neolithic nature cults, place it nearer to pantheism than to any kind of theism. Rather like Epicureanism in the West, Taoism in the classical age was more than anything else an ethical teaching on how to live wisely rather than how to fear or love the gods. Happy was the man of old who, without self-consciousness, without any sense of virtue, had followed the Tao. Then, as Chuang Tzu remarked in portraying the golden age of his imagination, "life on earth was full." Men "lived freely together, giving and taking, and did not know that they were generous. For this reason their deeds have not been narrated. They made no history."

Taoism, in other words, was a retrogressive faith; it looked backward to Paradise rather than forward to Heaven. Certainly it is a long way from Chuang Tzu's vision of men falling away from history through the practice of *wu-wei* (or non-practice—it is all the same) into a world where the gods are not mentioned, to the eschatological vision of the fulfillment of history through the Parousia and the coming of Christ's Kingdom that was the other side to Merton's mystical vision of man receiving the friendship of God in that desert of the heart which is the eternal present.

A similar problem arises in connection with Zen. Daisetz Suzuki, certainly the leading authority for the West on the Japanese variants of Zen, had declared emphatically that it is in no way a mysticism. Merton is inclined to treat it as if it were, though in *Mystics and Zen Masters* he does show himself aware of the problem of definition in cases where non-theistic religions are involved. There is obviously no doubt when we are dealing with theistic religions like Hasidic Judaism, Sufic Islam, Sikhism or devotional variants of Hinduism like Vaishnavite *bhakti* that the Hound of Heaven hunts in all these wildernesses. But there remain the other traditions, from which the person of God is absent but which we still regard as spiritually oriented; and here, in an article on "Contemplation and Dialogue," Merton brings in a definition of contemplation that seems to overcome the difficulty.

> By contemplation here we mean not necessarily mysticism pure and simple, but at least the direct intuition of reality, the *simplex intuitus veritatis,* the pure awareness which is and must be the ground not only of all genuine metaphysical speculation, but also of mature and sapiential religious experience. This direct awareness is a gift, but it also normally presupposes the knowledge and practice of certain traditional disciplines.

Such a definition would include movements like Taoism and Zen, and so from this point we will regard them as contemplative but not mystical. It would also lead us very near to the intuitions which we usually describe as poetic or aesthetic inspiration, and in areas like Zen the practice of art in fact becomes part of the practice of contemplation.

Merton's interest in Zen lacked the archaicist tinge that marked his interest in classical Taoism. Zen was a still living movement that already—by the time it aroused his interest—had been publicized and somewhat misunderstood in the West. He was able to meet its best-known spokesman, Suzuki, and to debate with him in print. If he had not died in Bangkok, his *Asian Journal* would have ended with a visit to Japan so that he could encounter the Zen masters in the country where they still represented a living tradition.

One can again speculate on the personal reasons for Merton's interest. I think that here, as in the case of Chuang Tzu, the poet in Merton was attracted not only by the traditional connection between Zen practices and certain forms of Chinese and Japanese poetry and painting but also by the aphoristic wit and the "impudent paradox" that characterized Zen poetry and particularly the Zen *koan*, the outrageous dialogue between master and pupil that plays a similar role to the tales of mischievous saints among the Sufis. He himself began to practise Zen calligraphy, and in his last volumes of poems, as we shall see, he achieved an interesting combination of Zen anti-logic and western absurdism. He endeavoured to achieve what he himself once described as the great feat of Zen art, "by using a bare minimum of form, to awaken us to the formless." Zen, as he also said, was "deliberately cryptic and disconcerting" and — in art as much as in religion — it was a "direct attack on formalism." (*Zen and the Birds of Appetite*) All these qualities he sought to absorb into the writing of his later years.

Yet there were contradictions even at this level, largely because Merton was inalienably influenced by western culture. He could seek Zen as an ally in his rebellion against the heritage of Cartesianism: "the reification of concepts, idolization of the reflexive consciousness, flight from being into verbalism, mathematics and rationalization." He could assert that "Descartes made a fetish out of the mirror, which the self finds itself. Zen shatters it." (*Conjectures*) He could spend a great deal of space in *Mystics and Zen Masters* describing with approval the teaching of Hui Neng who in the Zen tradition destroyed the concept of the self as the pure mirror. But he still did so in the rational manner of a trained Thomist, an heir of the Aristotelian tradition. He wrote discourses; he did not propound *koans*. Yet what, in these discourses, he most approved in Zen showed the emergence of his underlying Augustinianism, for he remarked that Zen is "nondoctrinal, concrete, direct, existential, and seeks above all to come to grips with life itself, not with ideas about life." Finally — and here we come to the kind of contradiction that faces any writer who feels impelled to record in some way the contemplative life — there was the fact that: "For Zen, from the moment fact is transferred to a statement it is falsified. One ceases to grasp the naked reality of experience and one grasps a form of words instead."

Zen masters, as Merton pointed out, preferred to let their brilliantly paradoxical remarks float in the air, since to record them would be to devitalize them, yet — a further paradox — the literature of Zen, like the literature of Sufism, consists almost entirely of the recorded oral statements of the masters. To a man of letters such contradictions are perpetually intriguing.

A further attraction that Zen held for Merton undoubtedly came from the fact that it was a doctrine of liberation that flourished — particularly in Japan — in an extremely authoritarian society, and that in some ways Zen monasticism operated according to that society's arbitrary rules of power. He does not go into the ambiguous relationship between Zen and the samurai tradition, or the extent to which Zen and the state religion of Shinto merged into each other; after all, Catholicism has a multitude of such skeletons in its ancient cupboards. But he does describe in some detail — and not without approval — the authoritarian discipline of the Zen monasteries. Faced with assertions of similarities between Zen and Trappist disciplines, he sidesteps the issue by pointing out that there is no Zen vow of stability, so that the Zen monastery is in some ways nearer to a seminary for training contemplatives than a community of men dedicated to sharing a search for grace to the end of their days.

Yet one senses the Trappist mind at work when, after rhetorically questioning whether a strict discipline is in fact necessary "in order merely to bring one to a simple recognition that one can find the answer to life's problems by oneself, since they are right in front of one's nose," he proceeds to provide what looks like an oblique justification of the strict discipline he himself underwent in the days of his own novitiate in a pre-aggiornamento Trappist abbey.

> Since the work of getting rid of the "I" is in fact so difficult
> and so subtle as to be completely impossible without the help of
> others, the disciple must submit unconditionally to the most rigor-
> ous obedience and discipline. He must take without question and
> without murmur every possible difficulty and hardship. He must
> bear insult, weariness, labor, opprobrium. (*Mystics and Zen
> Masters*)

And one is reminded of the crisis points in Merton's own early
monastic career, of the points when he was driven to breakdown,
when he adds:

> One might almost say that one of the purposes of the Zen
> training is to push the monk by force into a kind of dark night,
> and to bring him as quickly and efficaciously as possible into a
> quandary where, forced to face and to reject his most cherished
> illusions, driven almost to despair, he abandons all false hopes and
> makes a breakthrough into a complete humility, detachment, and
> spiritual poverty. (*Mystics and Zen Masters*)

There is no doubt that Merton understood Zen unusually
well for an outsider; Suzuki once remarked that he grasped it with
a sharper intuition than any other western student. His discourses
on it are clear, and he tells us very capably what it is not, frankly
admitting that only experience can tell, in full existential detail,
what it is. He values the ruthless breaking down of mental barriers
that stand in the way of simple seeing, of awareness, of — to use a
word universal among Buddhists — mindfulness. Like Taoism,
Zen makes no differentiation between subject and object, so that
it sees no "Absolute Object"; what it does see, Merton remarks
with appropriate whimsicality, is "Absolute Seeing"; not the "I"
seeing, but seeing itself. Yet, he emphasizes, this is no matter of
mere introspection, just as the Buddhist liberation or "nirvana"
is not the mere annihilation which nineteenth-century westerners
imagined it to be. The true Zen enlightenment, according to the
masters, is found in action (though not in self-conscious activism).
And Zen liberation, far from being a death to reality, is "a kind
of super-consciousness in which one experiences reality, not indirectly . . . but directly. . . ." Once again, Merton is noting that
the contemplative, far from being life-denying, perceives an

authenticity in the real world that is lost to those whose minds are trapped in formulae and abstractions.

There are many points in Merton's essays where he seeks out resemblances between Christian thought and Zen or Taoist insights. For example, he points to a resemblance between the Buddhist doctrine of the void or *sunyata* as the contemplative's goal, and the *todo y nada* of St. John of the Cross. He finds, in the synonymity and interchangeability within Zen doctrine of the terms Being, Seeing and Acting, "a surprising Trinitarian structure that reminds us of all that is most characteristic in the highest forms of Christian contemplation." But it seems to me that in all this Merton is dealing in analogies too remote to be meaningful. Zen and other forms of Buddhism accompany Christian contemplation to the point of uncovering the inner self, of arriving at undifferentiated awareness, but the farther journey that the Christian mystic makes through his discovered and liberated Self towards God is in no way paralleled in these other traditions.

It is mostly from Zen's way of clearing the lens of awareness that Christians may learn. But Zen, which is intolerant of meditational method, offers very little in the way of recognized techniques. Its masters do not, like the Indian and Tibetan gurus, transmit esoteric truths in whispers. Their method—call it rather a way—is to force the pupil to think for himself, to make him discover his own truths, through examining the outrageous *koans* they present to him.

Like the Zen masters, Merton himself was doubtful of the value of the unassisted quest for truth, and looked to the assistance of wiser men. He had always sought the advice of his monastic superiors, the help of spiritual directors, and—when the situation arose—had been obedient; he himself, in turn, became a spiritual director for the novices under his charge from 1955 to 1965. He therefore was able to accept without the kind of difficulty a Protestant Christian might experience the Asian idea of the guru, the teacher without whose guidance the neophyte may find his way into spiritual disaster and even, in the more extreme cases, into insanity. The role of the Zen master seemed to him a natural and necessary one, and it is likely that, if he had chosen to spend a period in a Zen monastery, he would have accepted the discipline which (as he had heard) was less rigorous for a foreign pupil than for a Japanese.

But it was India he eventually reached, not Japan, and the Buddhists with whom he associated most closely, and in greatest numbers, even though for a relatively short period, were the Tibetan refugees. Merton was not "very open to Hindu religion, as distinct from philosophy," as he admitted in his *Asian Journal*, and he made little effort during his brief forty days in India to increase his knowledge. But, like so many of us, in those first few years of the Tibetans' exile, he was intrigued by the legend of them as a people more spiritually oriented than any other in the modern world. The kind of worldliness that in more recent years has marred one's admiration for some of the better known Tibetan religious leaders (the Dalai Lama himself being a notable exception) was not then evident, and one looked on all Tibetans with an unqualified respect and — if one knew them personally — with a kind of wondering affection as people who came from a society that many centuries of isolation had preserved in a purer and more pristine condition than our modern world. It was as if people had come to us out of the mediaeval centuries of faith, and had come bearing immense treasures of lost wisdom, for the expectations we had of the ancient learning the Tibetans could reveal to us were so great that they were doomed to some degree of disappointment, perhaps because we expected the wrong things.

Merton encountered the Tibetans in Delhi, in Dharamsala and in the Darjeeling area. He had three long meetings with the Dalai Lama, leader of the powerful Yellowhat Gelugpa sect, and he encountered leading lamas of the older Redhat sects, the Kargyupa and the Nyingmapa, mainly in little monasteries (gompas) in the hills around Darjeeling. With these monastic leaders he conversed almost entirely through interpreters. Given the disadvantages of this kind of communication, he learned basic truths about Tibetan Buddhism and he was able to confirm a good deal through conversations with English-speaking Tibetan laymen like Sonam Kazi and Lobsang Lhalungpa, who were knowledgeable in Mahayanist doctrine and ways of meditation.

He was impressed by the ordinary Tibetan people, and developed a somewhat exaggerated idea of their spirituality based on the number of old people he met walking on mountain paths around Dharamsala spinning their prayer wheels and muttering mantras. He does not seem to have understood how much of this was the kind of routine pietism he would have dismissed among Christians, or how rapidly, by 1968, the younger Tibetan refugees were becoming westernized — and hence secularized — in their attitudes.

The Asian Journal, in which Merton describes these encounters, reached publication in a version, edited by his friends, of the notebooks he filled while he was in Asia. It is considerably less polished and thematically arranged than the earlier published journals over whose publication Merton presided, but this very fact gives it a general spontaneity, in comparison with the deliberation of tone that marks with the pencil of afterthought so much of *The Sign of Jonas* and *Conjectures of a Guilty Bystander.* It is a more informal, and in some ways a more uncertain Merton, as well as an older one, that we encounter. But two Mertonian characteristics not diminished are the questing enthusiasm with which he follows whatever interests him, and the sensitivity with which he observes the world of creation that he loved, so that even in the descriptions of Calcutta something more than the immediately perceptible horror of the place emerges. He sees the terrible beauty behind it all, the humanity that hides in its despair, and he can say: "For the masses of Calcutta, you dimly begin to think, there is no judgment. Only their misery. And instead of being judged, they are a judgment on the rest of the world."

It rapidly becomes clear from *The Asian Journal* that the Tibetans, who are deeply jealous of their esoteric traditions, discoursed mainly in generalities with Merton. The Tibetan lamas are in fact the most skillful of meditative technicians, and, unlike the Zen masters, lay great emphasis on method; even the Dalai Lama told Merton that their way was a "combination of wisdom and method." Many of their meditational techniques, like many of their beliefs, do not derive from the basic Buddhism taught in the sixth century BC by Sakyamuni, the historical Buddha, but are external accretions, like the Tantrism derived from early mediaeval Shaivite Hindu practices and the occult techniques of power derived from the indigenous Bon religion which was a variant of central Asian shamanism.

Merton immediately sensed that some of these Tibetan techniques, like meditation on the mandala and many of the Tantric practices, would be as useless to him as Loyola's highly technical *Spiritual Exercises* had been. But he was fascinated by the way of direct realization which Tibetans call *dzogchen,* meaning roughly Great Perfection. Some of his lay advisers urged him to follow the path of *dzogchen,* but the Dalai Lama warned him not to think it would be simple or that it would save any of the difficulties of the spiritual ascent, and the other lamas, with characteristic professional self-protectiveness, assured him unanimously that the path was impossible without a master, an assurance Merton was disinclined to question. Nevertheless, he was in two minds about how far he should indeed go.

Early in his stay in Dharamsala he noted in his journal that he was "not exactly dizzy with the idea of looking for a magic master but I would certainly like to learn something by experience and it does seem that the Tibetan Buddhists are the only ones who, at present, have a really large number of people who have attained to extraordinary heights in meditation and contemplation." Then one reads the accounts of meeting after meeting with learned lamas, meetings filled with the geniality that so often permeates one's encounters with Tibetans, yet rarely seeming to get beyond theoretical generalities backed by the suggestion that if Merton wishes to learn more he must find himself a guru and settle down to a long and rigorously directed course of meditation using established techniques. There are really two points where these conversations seem to break into wider fields: during the meetings with the Dalai Lama when the comparative philosophies of eastern and western monasticism were discussed, and during Merton's meeting in the hills near Darjeeling with a Nyingmapa teacher, Chatral Rimpoche, where the two men achieved the kind of communion based on experience that Merton had hoped to find often in Asia. They talked for hours, and then reached the conclusion which for Merton was also a significant confession of the limits of his spiritual achievement:

... He said he had meditated in solitude for thirty years or more and had not attained to perfect emptiness and I said I hadn't either.

The unspoken or half-spoken message of the talk was our complete understanding of each other as people who were somehow *on the edge* of great realization and knew it and were trying, somehow or other, to go out and get lost in it — and that it was a grace for us to meet one another.

Even now, however, though Merton believed Chatral Rimpoche was the guru he would choose if he made such a choice, he was unsure. "But I don't know yet," he remarked, "if that is what I'll be able to do — or whether I'll need to."

All the time Merton was developing the conclusion that what the Tibetans had to offer — apart from the kind of wisdom that where it occurs goes beyond any method — was principally what he called "natural techniques," means of manipulating the senses and the mind to achieve certain states of consciousness. "The Tibetans," he remarked in a letter to the monks of Gethsemani, "have a very acute, subtle, and scientific knowledge of 'the mind' and are still experimenting with meditation."

In the end he did not need to study with Chatral Rimpoche, and this was not because he died a few weeks after meeting him but because of an insight that came between the two events, an insight that — appropriately for a poet — was as deeply aesthetic as it was spiritual. He went to Ceylon and one day drove up from Colombo to the old Buddhist site of Pollonnaruwa, a place that haunts the memory of everyone who has visited it, for there, in a kind of shallow natural amphitheatre, two colossal Buddhas were carved from the natural rock about eight centuries ago, one seated in the lotus posture and the other and more gigantic reclining in the samadhi posture, with a smaller figure — that of Ananda the faithful disciple — standing beside its head. Undoubtedly these two great artifacts of the Hinayanist tradition are among the best examples of Buddhist art anywhere in the world, and happily they are not transportable. Merton's sensitive photographs of the sculptures not only illustrate well his lucent verbal description but also help us to empathize with his emotion as he felt that here, at this point, standing before these great statues carved by long-dead artists, all he had come to seek was revealed in a single illumination.

> Looking at these figures I was suddenly, almost forcibly, jerked clean out of the habitual, half-tied vision of things, and an inner clearness, clarity, as if exploding from the rocks themselves, became evident and obvious. The queer *evidence* of the reclining figure, the smile, the sad smile of Ananda standing with arms folded (much more "imperative" than Da Vinci's Mona Lisa because completely simple and straightforward). The thing about all this is that there is no puzzle, no problem, and really no "mystery." All problems are resolved and everything is clear, simply because what matters is clear. The rock, all matter, all life, is charged with dharmakaya...everything is emptiness and everything is compassion. I don't know when in my life I have ever had such a sense of beauty and spiritual validity running together in one aesthetic illumination. Surely, with Mahabalipuram and Pollonnaruwa my Asian pilgrimage has become clear and purified itself. I mean, I know and have seen what I was obscurely looking for. I don't know what else remains but I have now seen and have pierced through the surface and have got beyond the shadow and the disguise. This is Asia in its purity, not covered over with garbage, Asian or European or American, and it is clear, pure, complete. It says everything; it needs nothing.

It is from this point that Merton abandons the idea of seeking the truths of Asia by trying to adopt and practise a way of monastic life that belonged outside his culture. For him the revealed truths of Christianity still pointed to the ultimate goal. But far from allowing such a conclusion to suggest a turning away from other religions, Merton realized that the world's condition made it more important than ever in the past for the great religions to reach the level of mutual understanding and mutual enrichment. In an address he gave in Calcutta in October 1968, he stressed the critical stage that had been reached in human existence by "the growth of a truly universal consciousness in the modern world." He warned that such a consciousness "may be a consciousness of transcendent freedom and vision, or it may simply be a vast blur of mechanized triviality and ethical cliché." And in the address he gave in Bangkok on the day of his death, he pointed to what he believed was the way to make sure that it was "transcendental freedom and vision" that would triumph. "The combination of the natural techniques and the graces and the other things that have been manifested in Asia and the Christian liberty of the gospel should bring us all at last to that full and transcendent liberty which is beyond mere cultural differences and mere externals — and mere this or that."

This was the last statement Merton made personally to the world, but his voice continued to speak in appropriate silence through the mass of work he left unpublished, and particularly through the ambitious verse cycle, *The Geography of Lograire,* which he had prepared for publishing when he started on his Asian journey and which appeared in 1969, the year after his death. Since the last book that appeared in his life, *Cables to the Ace* (1968), is much nearer to *The Geography* than it is to most of the material in his early books, it seems reasonable to consider them together.

During his Asian journey Merton was reading Herbert Marcuse as he prepared for that last Bangkok lecture (whose title was "Marxism and Monastic Perspectives"), and he noted in his journal one argument of Marcuse, evidently because it seemed to reflect a practice he had already begun to follow in the experimental poetry he was writing.

> Marcuse has shown how mass culture tends to be anticulture — to stifle creative work by the sheer volume of what is "produced," or reproduced. In which case, poetry, for example, must start with an awareness of this contradiction and *use* it — as anti-poetry — which freely draws on the material of superabundant nonsense at its disposal. One no longer has to parody; it is enough to quote — and feed back quotations into the mass consumption of pseudo-culture (*The Asian Journal*)

This kind of anti-poetical use of the "superabundant nonsense" of the modern world is one of the notable characteristics of both *Cables to the Ace* and *The Geography of Lograire.* In both books a great deal that characterized the old Merton has vanished. The poetry of the choir, with its joyous noisy psalms, has gone completely, and even the poetry of the desert, with its clear simplicity, hardly exists in a recognizable form. Metrical form, except as parody, is banished, and so, as Merton tells us in his anti-prologue to *Cables to the Ace*, are "rhythms, melody," and "pictures," by which he means his old stock-in-trade of religious and nature imagery. The poet "has changed his address and his poetics are on vacation."

What Merton does present in each of the two last books is a kind of discontinuous mosaic, between whose apparently separate items (there are 88 prose and verse fragments in *Cables to the Ace*) the reader is led to make his own connections. Formally, it is obvious that the poet has made a step forward into modernity, and where his early poems might be seen within a landscape defined by the Blake of *Songs of Innocence* on the one hand and the Eliot of *Four Quartets* on the other, these later poems seem much more at home in a terrain bounded by the Blake of the Prophetic Books and the Pound of the *Cantos*. In fact, the first item of *Cables to the Ace* ends with the Blakeian sentence, "We assist once again at the marriage of heaven and hell," and what Merton is really exploring in this "mosaic" are indeed the two potentialities—heavenly and infernal—of the modern world, that of "transcendental freedom and vision" and that of "mechanized triviality and ethical cliché."

Into *Cables to the Ace* all the inclinations of thought and all the influences we have discussed in the last three chapters find their way. The fraudulence and cruelty of the modern world provide a great amount of the content, and the Zen *koan* forms a model for many of the paradoxical and apparently nonsensical fragments of *vers libre* that are included. The tone hovers between the contemptuous and the ironic, and the ironic modulates between mockery and infinite sadness. And, as always in Merton, the aphorisms tend to proliferate, this time often in the form of Blakeian "proverbs."

> Love the inevitable! Hate alone is perfectly secure in its reasons.
> Over the door of Hell is written: "Therefore!"

> Follow the ways of no man, not even your own...

> Note to subversives: Uncle has two extreme right hands and means business.

The targets of Merton's wit — for wit almost in a Restoration sense is perhaps the dominant element in this volume — are varied and numerous. There is Joyce: "Finn, Finn/ Tribal and double" who "sinks his fin/ Again in his/ Own Wake." There is Marshall McLuhan: "Some may say that the electric world/ Is a suspicious village. . . ." There is Dylan Thomas: "The hidden lovers in the soil/ Become green plants and gardens tomorrow. . . ." There are the arid theological pedants: "The sayings of the saints are put away in air-conditioned archives"; and there are the all-too-sane researchers into human consciousness, pilloried in an outrageous fantasy of the controls getting mixed up so that the experimental rats push the levers and make the experimenters their living puppets. There is the mock pathos of "Original Sin (A Memorial Anthem for Father's Day)":

> Weep, weep, little day
> For the Father of the lame
> Experts are looking
> For his name . . .

and the mock smugness of "Give me a cunning dollar . . .":

> I want to carry
> Cracking new money
> That knows and loves me
> And is my intimate all-looking doctor
> Old costly whiteheaded
> Family friend . . .

Quietly the good is mingled with the phoney, though in smaller proportions, and significantly it emerges towards the end, into which the poem's purpose unobtrusively flows. Eckhart and Ruysbroeck appear. "*Gelassenheit,*" beginning "Desert and void . . .," is a true statement of Merton's vision of spiritual impoverishment, ending in the mood of *New Seeds of Contemplation:* "Once you become aware of yourself as seeker, you are lost. But if you are content to be lost you will be found without knowing it, precisely because you are lost, for you are, at last, nowhere." And "Slowly slowly/ Comes Christ through the garden" is one of Merton's best poems of the desert, the sad comment on a sad age, as Christ seeks the lost disciple and finds him sleeping.

The disciple will awaken
When he knows history
But slowly slowly
The Lord of History
Weeps into the fire.

The whole poem *Cables to the Ace* ends with the poet walking away from it, "hiding the ace of freedoms."

Cables to the Ace has faults, and they are largely those of experimenting with experimentation, of looking round for unconventional styles, which sometimes unconsciously produces a kind of archaic surrealism in which the juxtaposition of unrelated images just does not work. But such flaws appear rarely, and considered as the anti-poetic diagnosis of the world's ills, accompanied by a poetic prescription for its cure, *Cables to the Ace* fits well into the Merton canon, and perhaps a little more towards its didactic than its aesthetic side.

One of the experimental approaches of modernism and postmodernism in the arts has been to find some kind of replacement for the linear, representational approach. It is easier to do this in other arts than in literature. Music has always been independent of the need to *say* anything, and for the last sixty years painters have been operating in a free field where colour and form can be used for purposes ranging from the most meticulous of realism to the most abstract of non-representational patterns. In writing, the process is more difficult, since words have both precise meanings and connotations; that is their property, and therefore an abstract patterning of words, often tried, has always failed, mainly because it has left unused the major function of words.

This means that the poet who wishes to break away from conventionality has to manipulate not only the words themselves but also their connotations and the associations they provoke. He is working with words, but also with images, with myths, with dreams, and with at least the splinters of ideas. What he can avoid is the linear form of the narrative or the discourse. This is why the major poems of our century are not epic narratives like *The Iliad*, or allegorical projections of theology like *The Divine Comedy* and *Paradise Lost*, or philosophic meditations like *The Prelude*, or romantic fantasies like *The Idylls of the King*, or satirical picaresques like *Don Juan,* in all of which a *line* of events or of thoughts is followed. Instead, the comparatively few long poems of our age, like *The Waste Land* and Pound's *Cantos,* and *Finnegan's Wake* in its own special subterranean way, have used the non-chronological, non-consecutive approach. In such poems, or proses which are really poems, one no longer goes on a journey from starting point to destination, from premise to conclusion. One is involved, rather, in a kind of net where everything is linked together and the tension is uniform, running in all directions, without centre, without beginning or end.

One can also use the image of the survey map, where we are less concerned with the relationships between points on roads and railways than with the flow of contours by which the whole is united, and I think this the most appropriate image for Merton's principal experiment in the long poem *The Geography of Lograire.* In so far as it has a definite structural arrangement, it is like that of the mandala, arranged in four sections entitled South, North, East and West, with the content held within this quadrilateral structure. It can also be likened to the old Aztec dance of the Four Directions, placating the spirits of the cardinal points, which twenty-four years ago I still saw being danced by Indians on the Mexican plateau. Both mandala and dance are images that project the sense of an occult and almost pre-religious ritual that runs through the whole of *The Geography of Lograire.*

Merton gave the manuscript of *The Geography of Lograire* to his publisher, James Laughlin, just before his departure for Asia on the journey from which he would not return. In an appended note he described it as a "purely tentative draft of a longer work in progress," as "a beginning of patterns, the first opening of the dream." And he went on to say that "in this wide-angle mosaic of poems and dreams I have without scruple mixed what is my own experience with what is almost everybody else's."

The Geography is indeed a mosaic, and it is wide-angle in the sense that its content is derived from many times and many cultures, and particularly those so-called primitive cultures that we in the West have either deliberately destroyed or casually corrupted. There are few examples of composed poetry in the old Mertonian sense, and the only one that forms a complete sustained poem is the prologue to the second part ("North"), which is entitled "Why I Have a Wet Footprint on Top of my Mind" and which is a brief meditation on remembering the places of his secular New York past ("To begin a walk / To make an air / Of knowing where to go / To print / Speechless pavements / With secrets in my / Forgotten feet . . ."), the places and incidents out of which fragmentary impressions emerge to make up the surrealist pattern of an urban nightmare where Eros and Thanatos, Love and Death, are in endless conflict.

Vast stretches of *The Geography of Lograire* — in fact the greater part of the poem's length — are "found poetry" in the sense of being extracts from some of the many books Merton found time to read once he had given up the Mastership of Novices and retired to his hermitage. Sometimes he uses the narratives of travellers or anthropologists almost without change, but on other occasions he has rewritten them into free verse. The arrangement of the fragments is his own and usually skillful, so that the final effect is less that of the "mosaic" he announces than of a collage, an example of pastiche as a literary art.

Throughout the book there is a counterpointing of mood between our urban civilization and the other cultures. The section "South," for example, begins with a cleverly allusive satirical poem about the American South in which Cain and the Lamb appear to be friends, but when — reading between the words of a surrealist pattern of strung-together newspaper phrases — we are aware of the slaughter of the Lamb (= the Negro), the poem ends with the phrase, "One narrow lane saved Lamb's friend Paschal Cain," and we remember Merton's warning that in a crisis the white liberals will betray the Negro. But after a series of other poems presenting the mental sicknesses of the American South, we move into other souths: the south of Africa, the Mayan south of Mexico. A beautiful Bantu invocation for the sacrifice of blue bulls and a Hottentot animal legend are followed by extracts from missionary accounts of how to deal with recalcitrant converts, and later the ceremonials of pre-Columbian Mayans are juxtaposed to the accounts of the destruction of their culture by Bishop Landa and others. In each case there is the contrast between the pristine and the degenerate, the primitive religion that was good in its own terms and the pseudo-Christian substitute that is inauthentic because it was imposed, and represented no conversion from the heart.

Some of these documentary passages reveal — as found poetry often does — an unconscious sense for the beauty of words among people unconscious of literary art. The final section of "North" consists of extracts from Dr. James Law's manuscript account of the Kane Relief expedition of 1855. In its own way, it is a tale of the desert, of life on the extreme frontiers, of death starkly encountered (and averted), and there is in the prose that peculiar austere lucidity which characterizes the writings of Victorian scientific explorers and out of which Merton here and there concocts a passage of extraordinary poetic beauty. For example:

> We climbed to a graveyard
> High on the wet rock
> There bodies sleep in crevices
> Covered with light earth then stones
> Some were sailors from England
> And America
> Now asleep
> In this black tower
> Over Baffin's Bay
> Waiting, waiting
> In endless winter.
> We left them to their sleep
> Ran down to meet the living girls. . . .
>
> Two Indians on a rock
> Like an owl's cry
> Signalling . . .

And then there are the long extracts — in some ways the most moving passage of the poem — from accounts of Melanesian Cargo Cults at the end of "East" and — at the end of "West" — of the Ghost Dance cults among Indians of the American Northwest in the later nineteenth century.

The Cargo Cults, of which I encountered at least two variants surviving in Melanesia as late as 1972, were strange quasi-religious movements occurring over a vast area in New Guinea, the Solomon Islands and the New Hebrides, and arising in response to a belief that everything the whites brought in their ships was really intended for the native people, and that the latter had only to give up their missionary-inspired habits, throw away their money, reject the values Europeans had forced on them; then the Cargo would come flowing in response to the invocations of their local prophets. Though there were occasional variants (one island collected several thousand dollars with which they put in a bid to purchase President Lyndon Johnson) the pattern remained suprisingly constant over this large area of people speaking many languages.

The section dealing with Cargo was one of the few parts of *The Geography of Logroire* that Merton annotated, and his remarks on the subject are particularly valuable because they throw light on other sections of *The Geography:*

> Though all this may seem naive and absurd to western "civilized" people, I, in common with some of the anthropologists, try to spell out a deeper meaning. Cargo is relevant to everyone in a way. It is a way in which primitive people not only attempt by magic to obtain the goods they feel to be unjustly denied them, but also and more importantly a way of spelling out their conception of the injustice, their sense that basic human relationships are being ignored, and their hope of restoring the right order of things. If they want Cargo it is not only because they need material things but because Cargo will establish them as equal to the white man and give them an identity as respectable as his. But if they believe in Cargo it is because they believe in their own fundamental human worth and believe it can be shown in this way.

It is this belief in the fundamental human worth of all men that is the real leitmotif of *The Geography of Logroire.* Most men in the West have abandoned it for the follies represented by the newspaper headlines and advertisement slogans that Merton incorporates into long passages of the poem. But men and women like the Cargo Cultists and the Ghost Dancers, like the Ranters and the Moslem heretics described by Ibn Battuta who appear in other parts of the poem, have not surrendered themselves. They are all seeking, in the crumbling of their vulnerable traditional world, a true vision, as Merton knew the Shakers had done, and he respects their search and implicitly condemns those who mock and persecute them. In the Ranters especially — with their enthusiastic teachings of the Dark Side of God, and of Heaven and Hell existing among us, and of God as a loving and not angry being — he obviously caught a whiff of Blake, and he caught more than a whiff of the Pharisees in their persecutors:

> Then God does not hate? Not even sin?
> So heaven and hell are in Deptford, Woolwich,
>   Battersea and Lambeth?
>
> Burn him through the tongue!

One is fascinated by the sense of underlying relationships between apparent incongruities over time and space that permeates *The Geography of Lograire,* and even though one feels the poem might have done with more polishing, it is still likely to stand as one of those imperfect masterpieces whose very largeness and scope of conception becomes itself a poetic virtue. But the fact that Merton thought of it as only a fragment of a much larger work makes one question the ultimate viability of such a scheme, as we are also forced to question Marcuse's idea of the infinite resources available to the anti-poet. Once we accept such an idea, we face the problem of how to select from the great mass of bad and good print that offers itself. How, having elected for anti-poetry and thus abdicated poetic discrimination, can we select what may be antipoetically acceptable? Inevitably, we find ourselves bound to set up criteria of badness in anti-poetry. And when that comes we are back in the old game of reserving special subjects and a special language — even if an anti-language — for poetry.

The Geography of Lograire is impressive as an experiment in literary form; it is impressive because it also shows Merton searching out beyond the accepted world religions for the signs of spirituality among even primitive men, and recognizing the strange disguises under which the Spirit of God may choose to settle. But I suspect that if Merton had lived he would have given up the longer version of the poem which he planned, so as to write again verse less dominated by political and moral imperatives. He left a small collection entitled *Sensation Time at the Home,* which did not find publication until it was included in the *Collected Poems* of 1977, and in some of these, like "Night of Destiny," "Elegy for a Trappist," "Seneca and Origen" the old quiet Merton of the poems of the desert is asserting his survival as he celebrates in Origen the freedom of the heart and mind that wins hatred but in the end love, the freedom of a man like himself,

> Who thought he heard all beings
> From stars to stones, angels to elements, alive
> Crying for the Redeemer with a live grief.

Epilogue

"I do not have clear answers to current questions," said Thomas Merton in *Conjectures of a Guilty Bystander*. "I do have questions." There is indeed a sense in which one can regard his whole life as a question, for the contemplative does not ask questions only of men and of the world; his quest leads him to the very heart of existence within himself, and if he is a Christian he awaits there an even deeper answer.

To write on any person is inevitably both to quest and to question, and an account of a writer's work or his life like the present book inevitably leaves the reader — and the writer as well — with the sense of questions unanswered. Some questions cannot be answered. Some questions, perhaps, should not be asked. But they are still insistent, and the most important relate to the relevancy of the man to his times.

In this case they can be summarized baldly in the question: Was Thomas Merton an anachronism? What significance can a monk have in the world when the monastery is no longer an organic part of our society and when monasticism as we have known it for centuries is in disorder?

The question would have less relevance if we were considering a contemplative hermit content to retreat completely out of the world into solitary meditation, for in a way that is to place oneself out of time entirely. But Merton was not only concerned with what happened in time to the extent of writing about current political trends and thus becoming involved at least peripherally in the world of action. He was also — unlike the Zen monks and the ancient Taoists whom he admired — an eschatologist, believing in the Parousia as an event in time and in Christ as the Lord of History.

In a personal way Merton — like many people born in his generation — was a man dislocated by his times. It is difficult even for those who were born into our bomb-shadowed present to realize the sense of dread, the fear of imminent and irreversible disaster that overshadowed the minds of young men in the Thirties, the dread Louis MacNeice expressed wryly when he wrote:

> The glass is falling hour by hour, the glass will fall forever,
> But if you break the bloody glass you won't hold up the weather.

In that mood of ambient and monstrous insecurity the Catholic Church and the monastery seemed, to someone capable of solitude and celibacy, a still point in a tottering world. The world did not collapse, but the changes it underwent changed the Church also, breaking down its ancient conservatism, making it more open to liberalism and even political radicalism, turning its attentions towards the world's problems, wrenching its institutions.

There was one side of Merton that welcomed this change, as he committed himself to being something more than a mere monastic writer, as he attempted to relate his contemplative life to the world in which Christianity's historical destiny must be played out. The social and moral critic, the experimental writer, were reawakened; the believer reached out to the unbeliever and found in existentialism a shared desert. Merton's reclusion actually gave him some advantages in this changed role. It gave him a stance from which he could observe the world as an outsider, or at least as a man on the margin, and there is no doubt that much of the lucidity of his criticism came from seeing the world from this privileged viewpoint.

Merton defended this viewpoint eloquently — as we have seen — by his portrayal of the monk as a marginal man, and at no point in his career was he more insistent on this marginality than during his last Asian days. Remembering the mediaeval monasteries, and those of the Tridentine age in piously Catholic countries like Spain and Austria, where the monastery was often a securer place for a poor man than the lay world and where monasticism had its role in a conservative order, one realizes that Merton is speaking very personally, or at least in the terms of a rapidly changing world, when he presents the monk as one of those people "who dare to seek on the margin of society, who are not dependent on social acceptance, not dependent on social routine, and prefer a kind of free-floating existence under a state of risk." That is hardly a good portrait of an average monk during most of the history of monasticism, whether Christian or Buddhist or Hindu. But it is a good portrait of the poet, of the true mystic, of the man whose life brings him into extreme situations, of the existentialist "who accepts the basic irrelevance of the human condition, an irrelevance which is manifested above all by the fact of death," and whose office it is "to go beyond death even in this life, to go beyond the dichotomy of life and death and to be therefore, a witness to life."

Out of this contradiction between routine monasticism and Merton's vision, there does indeed emerge a kind of quintessential vision of the original ideal of the monastery, which began as a withdrawal from society but has rarely failed to be betrayed by its own institutionalism so that it ends by becoming a part of the very world it rejects, as it did in mediaeval and much of modern Catholic Europe and also in the Tibet of the recent past.

Merton had liberated himself by the later 1950s from the narrow views he took with him into Gethsemani, and there is no doubt of the sincerity of his conviction when during the late 1950s he noted in the journal that became *Conjectures of a Guilty Bystander* that "my Church guarantees me the highest spiritual freedom. I would not be a Catholic if I did not believe this." Yet he did not escape from all the kinds of unfreedom that belonging to an ancient institution can incur.

We have already seen the contradictions in his attitude towards obedience and authority, and towards institutions he was equally ambivalent. It is true that, looking at what has happened to Christians in many parts of the world, he accepts the perishability of structures. "You cannot rely on structures," he said in that final Bangkok speech. "They are good and they should help us, and we should do the best we can with them. But they may be taken away, and if everything is taken away, what do you do next?" And, thinking in terms of a possible diaspora, he declared that "what is essential to monastic life" is not contained in buildings or clothing or even a rule. "It is concerned with this business of total inner transformation. All other things serve that end."

Yet, though he might see the monk as a marginal man, and foresee the dissolution of monastic structures, and doubtless be prepared to become a kind of spiritual displaced person if the need arose, Merton clung to Gethsemani with the kind of emotion that attaches one to a home, a family, a native landscape. And of course it was all these things to him, and also the place of refuge where he had become inwardly whole and had been able to follow and reconcile the dual vocations that shaped his life. He went to Asia with a certain relief at the idea of getting away from Gethsemani, but very soon he was feeling a nostalgia for the place and its shadowing hills, and noting down: "It is my monastery and being away has helped me to see it in perspective and love it more." (*The Asian Journal*)

Once, when Merton was Master of Novices, a postulant from Colombia came up to him in the novitiate garden. They looked at the evening beauty of the landscape, and then they went on to discuss Colombia, and the postulant said to Merton: "Why would not you, Father Merton, leave here and come to South America and start a totally new kind of monastic order, one that would appeal more to men of modern times?" And Merton commented, when he noted down the conversation in *Conjectures of a Guilty Bystander,* "I could not tell him how much I would like to try it, or how impossible it would be to make any such attempt without leaving the Order, and how impossible it would be for me to try to leave the Order." He remained, and he defended much that was traditional, even though it made him a "guilty bystander."

What have I proved by all this? Mainly that Merton was a man of apparently contradictory impulses, shaped by a past he was unable to escape entirely, yet capable of looking clearly at the world and at himself. Does that make him an anachronism?

Surely it makes him very much a man of our times, a man subject to yet aware of the plurality of all things, a man who had rejected linear and simplistic solutions because he was aware that "liberty is bound up with imperfection, and that limitations, imperfections, errors are not only unavoidable but also salutary." (*Conjectures*) He believed — and in this again he resembled Marx — that one respected the pluralities without making them ends in themselves, and sought to go beyond them. "We accept the division, we work with the division, and we go beyond the division."

It was of course this recognition of the need to respect the pluralities and to create a new reality by going beyond them that led Merton on his quest for dialogue and reconciliation between the separated brethren of Christianity and between Christians and those of other creeds who shared so much with them in spiritual self-realization. Perhaps we shall in time see his work for the reconciliation through understanding on a spiritual level of East and West as his principal contribution to the age in which he lived.

If we do, it will not be entirely fortunate, for the Merton who went to Asia after the twenty-seven years of his monastic experience was a man of many facets and yet, essentially, not a divided man, for he had learned how to bring his two vocations of poet and monk into a fruitful symbiosis. He may indeed have learned something more in the way of inner unity, for there is a very interesting passage in *Conjectures of a Guilty Bystander* where he remarks that the monk only becomes a true monk when he goes beyond the ideology of monasticism. He continues:

> In the same way, the true philosopher and the true poet become what they are when they "go beyond" philosophy and poetry, and cease to "be philosophers" or to "be poets." It is at that point that their whole lives become philosophy and poetry — in other words, there is no longer any philosophy or any poetry separable from the unity of their existence. Philosophy and poetry have disappeared. The ordinary acts of everyday life — eating, sleeping, walking, etc., become philosophical acts which grasp the ultimate principles of life in life itself and not in abstraction. (*Conjectures*)

Was this an ideal? Or did Merton himself achieve it? I suspect that in the later years in his hermitage, when his two vocations were in balance and fully active, and when he lived close to nature and blessed with friendships, he may well have done so. For one does not have the sense of a life whose promises were broken by his sudden death. On the contrary, the journey to Asia was in many ways a resolution, of hopes, of expectations, of ideas, an advance into reality expressed in the wisdom of his final speeches. Perhaps there was a gleam of unconscious prophecy in the final line of his late poem, "Night of Destiny": "In my ending is my meaning."

Bibliography

BOOKS BY THOMAS MERTON

The Ascent to Truth. New York: Harcourt, Brace and Company, 1951.

The Asian Journal of Thomas Merton. Edited by Naomi Burton, Patrick Hart and James Laughlin; consulting editor Amiya Chakravarty. New York: New Directions Publishing Corporation, 1973.

Basic Principles of Monastic Spirituality. Trappist, Kentucky: Abbey of Our Lady of Gethsemani, 1957.

The Behavior of Titans. New York: New Directions Publishing Corporation, 1961.

Bread in the Wilderness. New York: New Directions Publishing Corporation, 1953. Reprint 1960.

Breakthrough to Peace. Edited and with an introduction by Thomas Merton. New York: New Directions Publishing Corporation, 1962.

Cables to the Ace; or, Familiar Liturgies of Misunderstanding. New York: New Directions Publishing Corporation, 1968.

Cistercian Life. Spencer, Massachusetts: Cistercian Book Service, 1974.

Collected Poems. New York: New Directions Publishing Corporation, 1977.

Conjectures of a Guilty Bystander. Garden City, N.Y.: Doubleday & Co., Inc., 1966. Reprint 1968.

Contemplation in a World of Action. Introduction by Jean Leclercq. Garden City: Doubleday & Co., Inc., 1971. Reprint 1973.

Contemplative Prayer. New York: Herder and Herder, 1969. Reprint Garden City: Doubleday & Co., Inc., 1971. Reprints of *The Climate of Monastic Prayer*. Cistercian Studies, No. 1. Spencer, Massachusetts (Kalamazoo, Michigan): Cistercian Publications, Inc., 1969.

Disputed Questions. New York: Farrar, Straus and Giroux, 1960. FSG paperback reprint, 1976.

Early Poems / 1941-42. Anvil Press Publications, no. 9. Lexington, Kentucky: Anvil Press, 1971.

Emblems of a Season of Fury. New York: New Directions Publishing Corporation, 1963.

Exile Ends in Glory: The Life of a Trappistine. Milwaukee: Bruce, 1948.

Faith and Violence: Christian Teaching and Christian Practice. Notre Dame, Indiana: University of Notre Dame Press, 1968.

Figures for an Apocalypse. New York: New Directions Publishing Corporation, 1948.

Gandhi on Non-Violence. Edited and with an introduction by Thomas Merton. New York: New Directions Publishing Corporation, 1965.

The Geography of Lograire. New York: New Directions Publishing Corporation, 1969.

He Is Risen. Niles, Illinois: Argus Communications, 1975.

Ishi Means Man: Essays on the Native American Indian. Greensboro, S.C.: Unicorn Press, Inc., 1976.

The Last of the Fathers: Saint Bernard of Clairvaux and the Encyclical Letter, Doctor Mellifluus. New York: Harcourt, Brace and Company, 1954.

Life and Holiness. Garden City: Doubleday & Co., Inc., 1963.

The Living Bread. New York: Farrar, Straus and Giroux, 1956.

A Man in the Divided Sea. New York: New Directions Publishing Corporation, 1946.

The Monastic Journey. Edited by Patrick Hart. Kansas City: Sheed, Andrews & McMeel, 1977.

Monastic Orientation. Lectures Given to the Choir Novices at the Abbey of Gethsemani, 1950. Trappist, Kentucky: Abbey of Our Lady of Gethsemani, 1950.

Monks Pond. Quarterly edited by Thomas Merton. Nos. 1 to 4, Spring to Winter. Trappist, Kentucky: Thomas Merton, 1968.

My Argument with the Gestapo: A Macaronic Journal. Garden City: Doubleday & Co., Inc., 1969. Reprint New York: New Directions Publishing Corporation, 1975.

Mystics and Zen Masters. New York: Farrar, Straus and Giroux, Inc., 1967. Reprint New York: Delta Books, 1969.

The New Man. New York: Farrar, Straus and Giroux, 1961. FSG paperback, 1978.

New Seeds of Contemplation. New York: New Directions Publishing Corporation, 1962. Reprint 1972.

No Man Is an Island. New York: Harcourt, Brace and Company, 1955. Reprint Garden City: Doubleday & Co., 1967.

Opening the Bible. Collegeville, Minnesota: Liturgical Press, 1970.

The Plague, by Albert Camus. Introduction and commentary by Thomas Merton; general editor Lee A. Belford. New York: The Seabury Press, 1968.

Raids on the Unspeakable. New York: New Directions Publishing Corporation, 1966.

Redeeming the Time. London: Burns and Oates, 1966.

Seasons of Celebration. New York: Farrar, Straus and Giroux, Inc., 1964.

The Secular Journal of Thomas Merton. New York: Farrar, Straus and Giroux, 1959. FSG paperback, 1977.

Seeds of Contemplation. Norfolk, Connecticut: New Directions Publishing Corporation, 1949. Revised edition 1949.

Seeds of Contemplation. British revised edition London: Hollis and Carter, 1950.

Seeds of Destruction. New York: Farrar, Straus and Giroux, Inc., 1964.

Selected Poems. Introduction by Mark van Doren. New York: New Directions Publishing Corporation, 1959.

Selected Poems. Enlarged edition; introduction by Mark van Doren. New York: New Directions Publishing Corporation, 1967.

The Seven Storey Mountain. New York: Harcourt, Brace and Company, 1948. Reprint New American Library, n. d.

The Sign of Jonas. New York: Harcourt, Brace and Company, 1953. Reprint Garden City: Doubleday & Co., Inc., 1956.

Silence in Heaven. London: Studio Publications, 1956.

The Silent Life. New York: Farrar, Straus and Giroux, 1957. FSG paperback, 1975.

Spiritual Direction and Meditation. Collegeville, Minnesota: Liturgical Press, 1960.

The Strange Islands: Poems. New York: New Directions Publishing Corporation, 1957.

Thirty Poems. Norfolk, Connecticut: New Directions Publishing Corporation, 1944.

Thomas Merton on Peace. Edited and with an introduction by Gordon Zahn. New York: McCall Publishing Company, 1971.

A Thomas Merton Reader. Edited by Thomas P. McDonnell. New York: Harcourt, Brace and Company, 1962.

A Thomas Merton Reader. Revised edition edited by Thomas P. McDonnell. Garden City: Doubleday & Co., Inc., 1975.

Thoughts in Solitude. New York: Farrar, Straus and Giroux, 1958. FSG paperback, 1976.

The Waters of Siloe. New York: Harcourt, Brace and Company, 1949. Reprint Garden City: Doubleday & Co., Inc., 1962.

The Way of Chuang Tzu. New York: New Directions Publishing Corporation, 1965.

What Are These Wounds? The Life of a Cistercian Mystic, St. Lutgarde of Aywières. Milwaukee: Bruce, 1950.

The Wisdom of the Desert: Sayings from the Desert Fathers of the Fourth Century. Translated by Thomas Merton. New York: New Directions Publishing Corporation, 1960.

Zen and the Birds of Appetite. New York: New Directions Publishing Corporation, 1968.

Permissions

Every effort has been made to determine who owns the copyright on any material used in this book. Apologies are tendered in advance to proprietors and publishers.

Grateful acknowledgement is hereby given for permission to quote from the following works of Thomas Merton:

The Asian Journal. Copyright© 1968, 1970, 1973 by the Trustees of the Thomas Merton Legacy Trust. Reprinted by permission of New Directions Publishing Corporation, New York.

Bread in the Wilderness. Copyright 1953 by Our lady of Gethsemani Monastery. Reprinted by permission of New Directions Publishing Corporation, New York.

Collected Poems. Copyright© 1977 by The Trustees of the Merton Legacy Trust. Reprinted by permission of New Directions Publishing Corporation, New York.

Conjectures of a Guilty Bystander. Copyright© 1965, 1966 by The Abbey of Gethsemani. Reprinted by permission of Doubleday & Company, Inc.

Contemplation in a World of Action. Copyright© 1965, 1969, 1970, 1971 by The Trustees of the Merton Legacy Trust. Reprinted by permission of Doubleday & Company, Inc.

Contemplative Prayer. ©Doubleday & Company, Inc., 1971. Reprinted thanks to Cistercian Publications, Inc., publishers of the original edition, *The Climate of Monastic Prayer*, 1969.

Gandhi on Non-Violence. Copyright© 1964, 1965 by New Directions Publishing Corporation. Reprinted by permission of New Directions Publishing Corporation, New York.

Index